PRAISE FOR *THE SKETCHNOTE*

"Entertaining and memorable (just like sketchnotes), this fast-reading,
fact-packed book by the godfather of sketchnoting provides everything
you and your team need to know about the creative, mnemonic,
and business benefits of this brilliant new method of note taking."
—Jeffrey Zeldman, author of *Designing with Web Standards*

"Mike Rohde has taken his original, fun, and smart approach
to note taking and broken it down into simple, clear steps.
Now anyone can use sketchnotes to capture ideas—even you and me."
—Chris Guillebeau, author of *The $100 Startup*

"Sketchnotes are a great way to capture the highlights of an idea
in a way that will naturally work for your brain.
Nobody will teach you how to do it better than Mike."
—David Heinemeier Hansson, co-author of *REWORK*

"*The Sketchnote Handbook* is an informative, hands-on book
designed to quickly share the principles of sketchnoting
so you can get right to creating sketchnotes for yourself. Mike's fun,
illustrative style energizes you to pick up a pen and sketchnote!"
—Nancy Duarte, CEO Duarte Inc.,
and best-selling author of *Resonate* and *Slide:ology*

"Never fear note taking again. Mike Rohde demystifies the practice
and makes it accessible to everyone. Your brain will thank him later."
—Sunni Brown, co-author of *Gamestorming* and leader of the Doodle Revolution

"This book is not really a book. It's a tool kit for learning a new and better
way of capturing and understanding information, and it's perfectly aligned
with the way our brains actually work. If you're a student, teacher, or businessperson,
this book has the potential to change the way you learn, and the way you think."
—Daniel Coyle, *The New York Times* best-selling author of
The Talent Code and *The Little Book of Talent*

"The perfect introduction to visual note taking
and the most useful how-to guide I've ever read, no contest."
—Josh Kaufman, author of *The Personal MBA: Master the Art of Business*

the Sketchnote HANDBOOK

→ THE ILLUSTRATED *guide* ←
to Vi$ual NOTE TAKING

by MIKE ROHDE
the illustrator of REWORK

THE SKETCHNOTE HANDBOOK:
The illustrated guide to visual note taking

Mike Rohde

Peachpit Press
Peachpit Press is a division of Pearson Education.

Acquisitions Editor: Nikki Echler McDonald
Development Editor: Anne Marie Walker
Proofreader: Liz Welch
Production Editor: Katerina Malone
Indexer: James Minkin
Cover Design and Illustrations: Mike Rohde
Interior Design and Illustrations: Mike Rohde

THAT'S MY A-TEAM!

ISBN 13: 978-0-321-85789-7
ISBN 10: 0-321-85789-5

10 17

Printed and bound in the United States of America

To Gail, Nathan, Linnea, and Landon,
thank you for your support on this
long and challenging journey.

You are the reason I work so hard
to create things and share my ideas.

I love you.

ACKNOWLEDGMENTS

TAKING ON A PROJECT OF THIS MAGNITUDE is a great reminder of just how valuable my family, friends, colleagues, and community are. Without them, I'm certain *The Sketchnote Handbook* would not have happened.

GAIL, you are the first and most important person on the list. Even though you were expecting a baby, you encouraged and supported me on many late nights and weekends. Thanks for sharing the vision with me. I love you!

NATHAN, LINNEA AND, LANDON, thanks for supporting me during the creation of the book. As your dad, I hope my work makes you proud.

VON GLITSCHKA, you get credit for sparking this book over Thai food in Portland. Thanks for believing in me and pitching my book idea just minutes after dinner.

NIKKI MCDONALD, you've been behind me on this book from the beginning to the end. Thanks for considering my book idea, selling it to your team, and keeping me on track and encouraged through the long, hard creation process. Most important, thanks for helping me create something truly unique and different.

ANNE MARIE WALKER, you've been a fabulous editor, challenging me to make the book better. Thanks for keeping me on my toes and making my prose look so good.

PEACHPIT, your team has been a joy to work with. Everyone was professional and so easy to work with. Thank you Nancy, Glenn, Katerina, Mimi, Lupe, Charlene, Amy, Eric, Liz, and James for making my first book experience a great one.

DAVID FUGATE, thanks for your expert guidance through the book contract process. I couldn't have asked for a better agent.

DELVE WITHRINGTON, thanks for creating fonts of my hand lettering. Your typefaces have saved me many long hours of drawing every letter by hand.

FEATURED SKETCHNOTERS: Binaebi Akah, Craighton Berman, Boon Chew, Veronica Erb, Jessica Esch, Alexis Finch, Michelle George, Eva-Lotta Lamm, Gerren Lamson, Matthew Magain, Timothy Reynolds, Francis Rowland, Chris Shipton, Paul Soupiset, and Kyle Steed, thanks for your contributions.

BRIAN ARTKA, GABE WOLLENBURG, STEPHEN MORK, MARK FAIRBANKS, AND CYNTHIA THOMAS, thanks for your encouragement throughout the project.

JON MUELLER, thanks for allowing my sketchnotes of your talk to become such a key part of the book. I've been honored to call you a friend and appreciate your guidance in the creation of my first book.

FRIENDS AND COLLEAGUES , thanks for your reviews and feedback about the book in production. This is a better book because of your help.

TO THE SKETCHNOTING COMMUNITY, thanks for your support through the years. I'm excited to see where our community will go and how it will grow once this book reaches new readers and viewers.

ABOUT THE AUTHOR

MIKE ROHDE has a passion for simple and usable design solutions. That passion, along with his lifelong habit of recording concepts and observations through sketching and doodling, inspired him to develop sketchnotes—a practical art that translates simple and complex ideas into easily recalled bits of information.

Professionally, Mike focuses on user interface, user experience, visual design, and icon design for mobile and web applications at *Gomoll Research + Design* in Milwaukee, Wisconsin.

As a sketchnoter, Mike provides live, real-time sketchnotes of events, meetings, and experiences in venues across the United States.

In his illustration practice, Mike uses his unique drawing style to amplify and clarify ideas. His work has been featured in *REWORK*, the best-selling book by Jason Fried and David Heinemeier Hansson; *The $100 Startup*, a best-selling book by Chris Guillebeau; and *The Little Book of Talent* by Daniel Coyle.

Community and sharing are important cornerstones of Mike's philosophy, as evidenced by the creation of *The Sketchnote Army*, a website dedicated to finding and showcasing sketchnotes and sketchnoters from around the world.

Mike has also shared his thinking, design process, and samples of his design and illustration work at his personal website, rohdesign.com, since 2003.

Mike lives with his wife, Gail, and children, Nathan, Linnea, and Landon, just outside of Milwaukee. He's an avid Green Bay Packers fan.

Learn more about Mike at **rohdesign.com.**

CONTENTS

INTRODUCTION

IT WAS THE WINTER OF 2006 AND I COULDN'T TAKE IT ANYMORE.
I was done. Fed up. I vowed not to take another note with a mechanical pencil or with a giant notebook until I'd found a better way to take notes.

Thinking back, I'm not sure how note taking had become such a burden. In high school and college, I enjoyed expressing ideas visually—easily blending words with drawings, diagrams, and typography in my notebooks.

Somewhere in the process of growing up and getting a job, I lost my way. The relaxed, visual note-taking approach from my college days had morphed into a fanatically detailed, text-only death march. Ironically, I became a great note taker who couldn't stand taking notes.

The solution to my note-taking problem was a blank pocket Moleskine, stacked neatly on my bookshelf. I'd bought it on a whim a few months before and I realized that its small size, paired with an unerasable pen, could be a perfect way to challenge my overly detailed, note-taking mind-set.

In January 2007, I brought my Moleskine and a gel pen to Chicago for a conference to try sketchnoting. Could I take fewer but better notes? If I focused on quality, could I live with seeing my mistakes in pen? Would adding drawings to my notes bring back my joy of note taking? Could taking notes become fun again?

The answer to these questions was a resounding yes! As I captured my first sketchnotes, I was able to slow down and listen for big ideas. I loved the no-turning-back attitude of using a pen. Best of all, I had a great time taking notes again.

Ever since that mind-altering experience, I've been working hard through my blog, *The Sketchnote Army,* and at live presentations and workshops to share my passion for sketchnoting. I take great pleasure in talking about why sketchnoting enables you to take better notes, explaining how to create sketchnotes, and persuading people to give sketchnoting a try. This passion for sketchnoting is what drove me to spend hundreds of hours writing, illustrating, and designing this book. I want you to enjoy taking notes as much as I do, and I hope that by the end of this book you will.

WHO IS THIS BOOK FOR?

Whether you believe you can or can't draw, I'm here to tell you that anyone who can make marks on paper can benefit from this book. Sketchnotes are about hearing and capturing meaningful ideas, not how well you draw.

Take it from me, you can create sketchnotes. In this book, I will show you how to draw simple objects, create custom lettering, and use other hand-drawn elements to help you express your thoughts visually. Even if you can't draw a straight line, you can learn to sketchnote with a little practice.

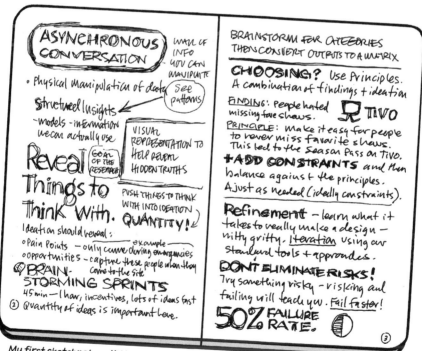

My first sketchnotes • UX Intensive 2007

WHAT IS *THE SKETCHNOTE HANDBOOK?*

The Sketchnote Handbook is a simple, visual manual designed to teach you basic sketchnoting concepts, approaches, and techniques quickly, so you can start creating sketchnotes immediately.

Each page of this book has been lovingly hand-sketched to show you how much fun it is to learn from notes that incorporate pictures and words equally. Rather than write a lot of words about sketchnoting, I decided that if I was going to talk the talk, I'd better walk the walk (or, maybe, sketch the sketch?). So, I created the entire book as one, long, fun—hopefully inspiring—illustration.

4 CREATE A TITLE

A completed title page, ready to go.

I like to use my iPhone to find photos of the speaker for reference on my title page.

ONCE I'VE SETTLED IN, I check the topic and the speaker's name, verify spellings, and sometimes find a photo on my phone to create a visually interesting title page for the speaker or the topic.

I complete my title before the speaker begins, so I can focus on the talk rather than rushing to create a title at the start of the presentation.

5 SKETCHNOTE

When the talk begins, I listen, synthesize the ideas I'm hearing, and start drawing what I'm thinking about as sketchnotes in my sketchbook.

A completed sketchnote.

6 PHOTOGRAPH

When I'm done sketchnoting, I shoot photos of my sketchnotes. This is a great way to immediately share what you've created via social media, and photos serve as a good backup of your sketchnotes.

I like to shoot each page as a single image. Photos of single pages provide more detail and are easy to view on mobile devices.

The Sketchnote Handbook · Chapter 4

THE SKETCHNOTE COMMUNITY

Of course, I'm not the only person in the world who sketchnotes. I'm amazed and energized by the wide variety of people all over the world who create and actively share their sketchnotes. I love the sense of community that has sprung up around this process, and I've made a great many friends through sharing and discussing sketchnotes online and at conferences.

I invited 15 of these friends—leading sketchnoters from around the world—to each create a two-page spread for this book that shares a bit about who they are, how they came to sketchnoting, and a tip or two to help you take better notes.

What I hope you'll notice from looking at their work at the end of each chapter is that everyone sees the world differently; everyone processes information differently; everyone has their own, unique style, and that's part of what makes sketchnoting so much fun! There's no right way or wrong way to do it.

I will teach you the basic principles of sketchnoting, but the real joy will come when you start creating sketchnotes and discover how taking notes can unleash your creativity and make paying attention, even at the most boring meetings, something you look forward to doing.

REACH OUT

As you learn from this book, I encourage you to share your own sketchnotes at *The Sketchnote Handbook* Flickr group (**www.flickr.com/groups/thesketchnotehandbook**). I plan on hanging out there a lot, and I'd love to see how you've taken this process and made it your own.

You can view more of my work and contact me through my personal website at **rohdesign.com** or on Twitter at **twitter.com/rohdesign**. I look forward to hearing what you think of the book and learning about your sketchnoting experiences.

IT'S TIME TO GET STARTED. GRAB A NOTEBOOK AND A PEN. LET'S GO TAKE SOME NOTES!

LET'S GO!

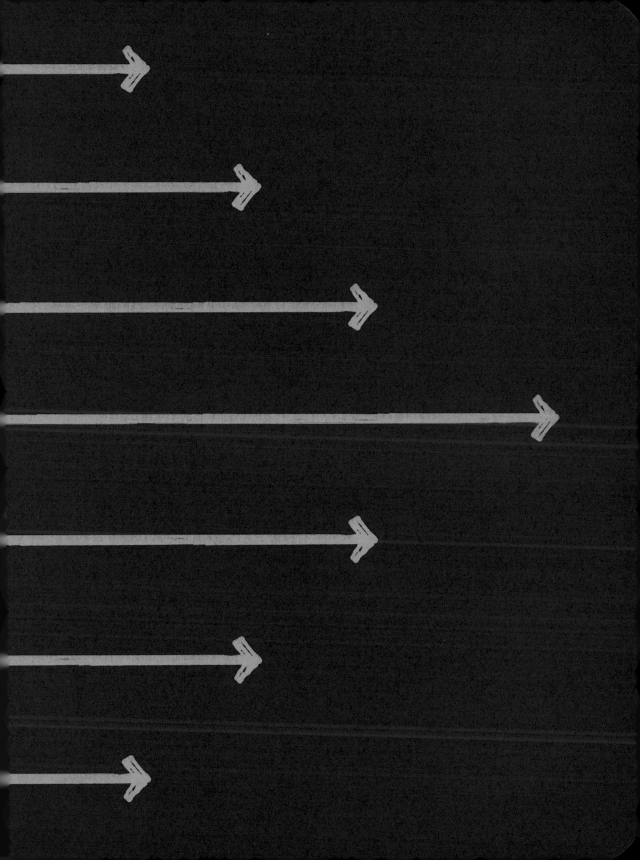

what are SKETCHNOTES?

SKETCHNOTES ARE RICH VISUAL NOTES CREATED FROM A MIX OF HANDWRITING, DRAWINGS, HAND-DRAWN TYPOGRAPHY, SHAPES, AND VISUAL ELEMENTS LIKE ARROWS, BOXES & LINES.

SKETCHNOTES WERE BORN of
frustration!

I WAS FRUSTRATED by the highly detailed, text-only notes I was taking at conferences and in meetings. The stress escalated as I worked hard to capture every last detail in very large, lined notebooks. Worse, I never looked at my notes after their completion.

ARG! I HATE THIS!

A PENCIL
I was so worried about making mistakes, I took my notes in pencil, so I could erase any errors.

A LARGE, LINED NOTEBOOK
Because I tried to capture every detail, I needed large pages to store all of that information.

I decided to
GIVE UP
— and —
TRY
Something
NEW.

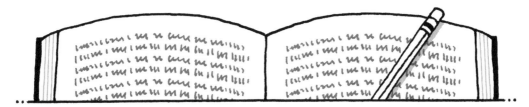

I relaxed a bit,

LISTENED

→ *more* ←

INTENTLY,

And
FOCUSED
ON CAPTURING
the BIG
IDEAS.

INSTEAD
of using a
PENCIL &
LARGE
NOTEBOOK

I *Limited*
MYSELF
TO A PEN &
A POCKET
MOLESKINE
SKETCHBOOK.

I CHALLENGED MYSELF
to write and draw notes more

deliberately.

○—————★—————○

THIS NEW WAY OF NOTE TAKING

was enjoyable AND **FUN!**

○—————○—————○

I was able to focus on the BIGGER PICTURE,
expressing CONCEPTS with drawings, type, and text.

Jon MUELLER

Handwriting helps describe concepts verbally.

* I COINED a NAME * for THIS PROCESS: Sketchnotes.

SKETCHNOTES AREN'T DRY AND DETAILED BUT ARE *Simple and Clear.*

My personality WAS BAKED INTO MY SKETCHNOTES LIKE CHOCOLATE CHIPS IN A BATCH OF *chocolate chip cookies.*

SKETCHNOTES are VISUAL *maps*

They're built from meaningful thoughts and ideas your mind collects and squirrels away during:

| TALKS | PANELS | Experiences |

THIS VISUAL and HOLISTIC APPROACH

to note taking engages your mind so you can understand
the ideas you're hearing while activating your hand
to turn those ideas into concrete, VISUAL NOTES.

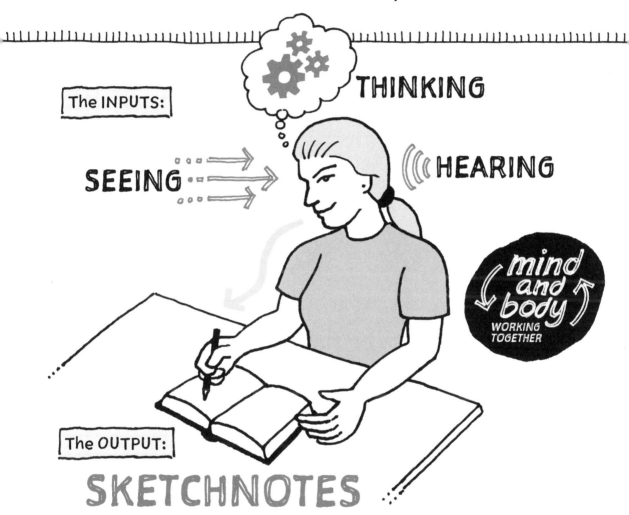

The INPUTS:

THINKING

SEEING

HEARING

mind
and
body
WORKING
TOGETHER

The OUTPUT:

SKETCHNOTES

BECAUSE YOUR MIND AND BODY ACT TOGETHER, YOU
CAN RECALL MORE OF WHAT YOU HEAR AND DRAW.

SKETCHNOTERS INFUSE THEIR OWN
SKETCHNOTES
WITH UNIQUE PERSONALITY

Craighton   Carolyn   Eva-Lotta   Austin

From drawing and handwriting style to the ideas included and *how* those ideas are expressed on the page.

THE RESULT?
EACH SKETCHNOTE IS UNIQUE,
EVEN THOUGH THE UNDERLYING PRINCIPLES
OF SKETCHNOTING REMAIN THE SAME.

How are sketchnotes CREATED?

the
HAN SOLO
MBA

SKETCHNOTES are created in real time while listening to a presentation, talk, or panel discussion.

To sketchnote, you listen closely to meaningful ideas, consider what they mean, and then create a visual map of them. The goal is to forgo the details and instead listen for big ideas that resonate, converting those ideas into visual notes that include both words and pictures.

Whether you create sketchnotes with pen and paper or digitally, the approach is the same.

Can you create sketchnotes?

YES. YOU. CAN!

MANY PEOPLE tell me they can't create sketchnotes because they can't draw. You can draw; you just need to awaken your grade school skills!

KIDS draw constantly!

They doodle ideas with ease and will draw what they imagine without a second thought.

GUESS WHAT?
You were a kid once:
I bet you drew like crazy.

KIDS DRAW
TO EXPRESS IDEAS.

They don't worry about how perfect their drawings are, as long as their

IDEAS
ARE CONVEYED.

the 5 Basic Elements

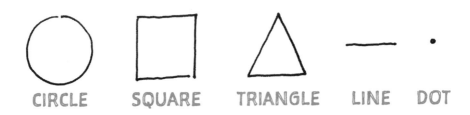

CIRCLE   SQUARE   TRIANGLE   LINE   DOT

EVERYTHING YOU WANT TO DRAW
CAN BE CREATED WITH THESE 5 ELEMENTS.

Can you identify the 5 basic elements in these simple drawings?

ONCE YOU REALIZE how the objects around you are made from these 5 elements, it becomes easier to draw all sorts of things.

IDEAS, NOT ART!

IDEAS, NOT ART!

Sketchnotes are about capturing and sharing ideas, not about art.

SKETCHNOTES ARE a WAY TO THINK ON PAPER USING IMAGES & WORDS.

ART

BAD DRAWING   GOOD DRAWING

VS.

Either way it's still a dog.

Even the roughest drawings can express ideas effectively.

○————○

INSTEAD OF WORRYING ABOUT WHAT
YOU CAN'T DRAW,
START WITH SIMPLE ITEMS
YOU CAN DRAW.

The chapters that follow and lots of practice
will help you build your drawing skills.

ONE STEP
AT A TIME.

WHEN YOU'RE STARTING ANYTHING NEW, IT MAKES SENSE TO TAKE IT SLOW & BUILD ON SUCCESS.

Take the first step: Reserve a small area in your regular notes to try some sketchnote techniques — even if it's a drawing of the speaker.

As you experiment and try out the simple techniques in this book, you can add more tools to your visual-thinking toolbox, and as a result, add more richness to your notes, one step at a time.

RECAP

→ Regular notes were frustrating, so I used drawings to help express the big ideas.

→ Setting limitations helped me become more deliberate with what I captured.

→ Sketchnotes are rich, visual notes that act as a map of the ideas you see and hear.

→ Keeping an active mind and body helps you engage and recall more detail later on.

→ Sketchnotes let you add your own personality, creating richer notes.

→ You can draw nearly anything using just a square, circle, triangle, line, and dot.

→ Sketchnotes are about ideas, not art!

→ One step at a time. Build on success.

★ **NEXT: WHY SKETCHNOTE?**

UX designer living in OHIO

@siriomi

Binaebi Akah

siriomi.com

z z z z

Began sketchnoting in a DESPERATE attempt staying awake during a grad school lecture

But now I love it because it engages my mind and triggers my memory

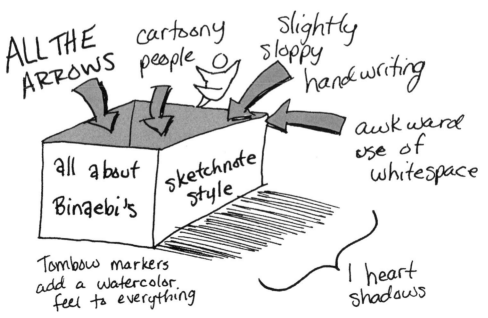

ALL THE ARROWS

cartoony people

Slightly sloppy handwriting

all about Binaebi's

sketchnote style

awkward use of whitespace

Tombow markers add a watercolor feel to everything

I heart shadows

Tips & Tricks

 Listen for the things that make you nod, frown, smile...

 that means something resonated!

always draw the head first when drawing people

it gives you a scale to work with!

Le Pen is my **current** favorite

☑ micron
☑ ball point
☑ sharpie pen
☑ prismacolor pen

doesn't bleed

smooth writing

quickly dries

the **CANSON** wire-bound hardcover sketchbook

1. can draw in my lap
2. Easy to flip pages

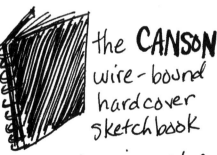 I draw heart balloons over my "unfixable" mistakes

JUST KEEP DRAWING! ♡ all your mistakes

CRAIGHTON BERMAN

I'M PRIMARILY INTERESTED in **IDEAS**

INVENTION

INNOVATION CONSULTANT

DESIGN ENTRE-PRENEUR

VISUAL THINKING

ILLUSTRATOR

IDEA-DRIVEN PRODUCTS

CHICAGO ILL.

FIRST SKETCHNOTE: **1986**
BUSTED for DOODLING on MY DESK in FIRST GRADE

WHY DO I SKETCH NOTE?
OVER-ACTIVE IMAGIN-ATION.

CRAIGHTON BERMAN.COM
TABLET NOTES

iPAD NOTES
FUELEDBY COFFEE.COM

LARGE SCALE GRAPHIC RECORDING

AND of COURSE in A SKETCH BOOK!
(OLD SCHOOL)

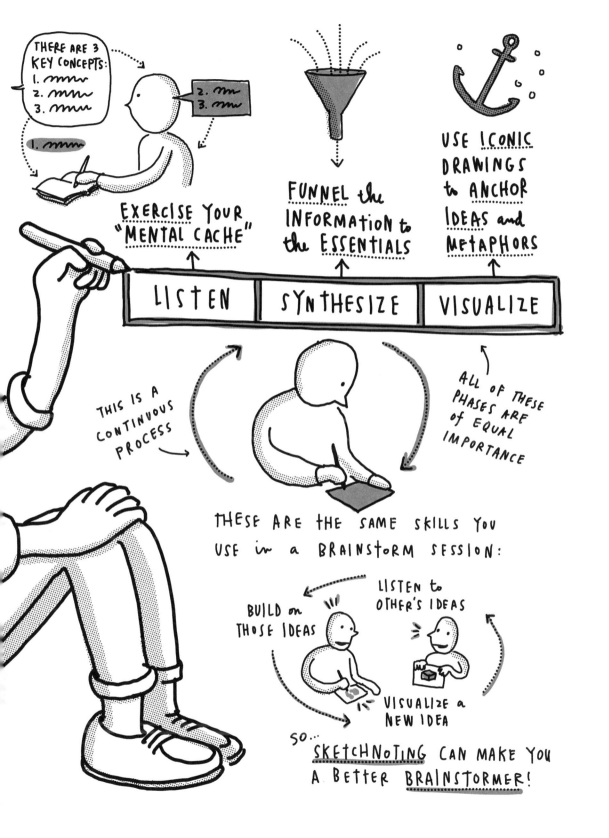

CHAPTER 2

WHY SKETCHNOTE?

WHY SPEND EXTRA EFFORT CREATING SKETCHNOTES IF PLAIN OL' TEXT NOTES ARE GOOD ENOUGH? BECAUSE SKETCHNOTING ENGAGES YOUR BRAIN IN MORE WAYS THAN PLAIN NOTES CAN, and THEY HELP YOU REMEMBER MORE DETAIL.

SKETCHNOTING *Engages*
→ YOUR WHOLE MIND ←

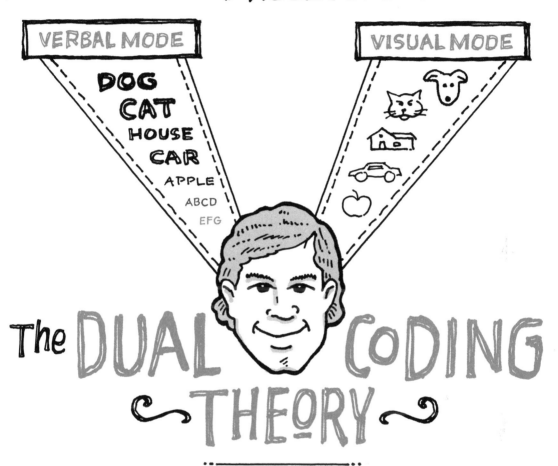

VERBAL MODE

DOG
CAT
HOUSE
CAR
APPLE
ABCD
EFG

VISUAL MODE

The DUAL CODING THEORY

THE DUAL CODING THEORY,
proposed in the 1970s by Allan Paivio,
suggests that the brain processes information
using two primary channels: verbal and visual.

 ★VERBAL★
Concepts as words

 ★VISUAL★
Concepts as images

WHEN BOTH MODES are ACTIVE,
YOUR BRAIN CREATES AN ASSOCIATIVE
LIBRARY of WORDS and IMAGES with MENTAL
CROSS-REFERENCES BETWEEN THEM.

SKETCHNOTING activates verbal and visual modes to capture concepts. **YOUR WHOLE BRAIN** is absorbed in hearing, synthesizing, and seizing ideas.

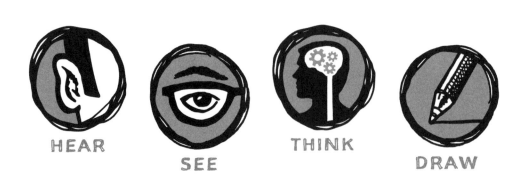

HEAR
SEE
THINK
DRAW

SKETCHNOTING CREATES A
VISUAL MAP

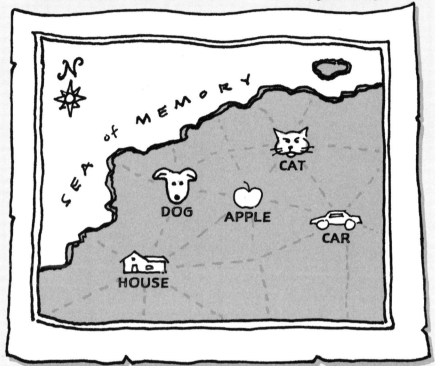

When your brain codes verbal and visual concepts together, it's also building a visual map of what you are hearing, seeing, and thinking.

◁————————○————————▷

ENGAGING your whole brain has other positive effects, like improving your memory and recall.

THE VISUAL MAP YOU CREATE

can help you recall the details of a presentation. I often recall thoughts, feelings, and other details when viewing my sketchnotes.

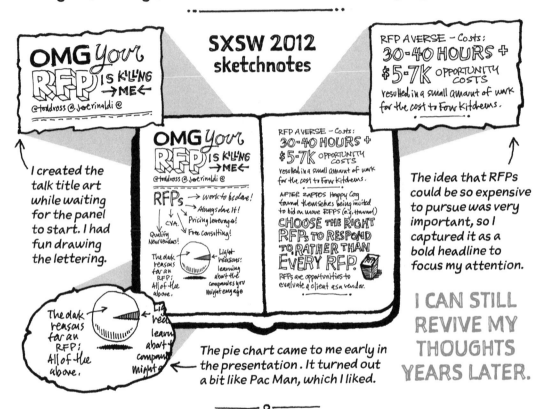

SXSW 2012 sketchnotes

OMG *your* RFP IS KILLING →ME← @toddross @joerinaldi @

RFP AVERSE – Costs: 30-40 HOURS + $5-7K OPPORTUNITY COSTS resulted in a small amount of work for the cost to Four Kitchens.

I created the talk title art while waiting for the panel to start. I had fun drawing the lettering.

The idea that RFPs could be so expensive to pursue was very important, so I captured it as a bold headline to focus my attention.

I CAN STILL REVIVE MY THOUGHTS YEARS LATER.

The pie chart came to me early in the presentation. It turned out a bit like Pac Man, which I liked.

IN AN EXAMPLE STUDY, a group of 40 volunteers listened to a monotonous 2-minute phone message. 20 of the participants shaded boxes while listening, the other 20 simply listened.

IN A SURPRISE QUIZ THAT FOLLOWED, THE GROUP OF 20 DOODLERS RECALLED 29% MORE THAN THE NON-DOODLERS.

Source: The Guardian, Feb 26, 2009

SKETCHNOTING HELPS *your* CONCENTRATION.

CREATING SKETCHNOTES from the ideas you are hearing helps focus your mind on the present moment.

When your mind and body are working in tandem, there is little room left for distractions.

As you practice
and improve
your sketchnoting
techniques,
LISTENING
and **DRAWING**
at the same time
will feel more
natural.

WHEN I SKETCHNOTE,
I'm completely engaged with what
I'm listening to and turning into

sketchnotes.

The focused activity of listening, analyzing ideas,
and mapping those ideas on paper puts me
→ IN A ZONE ←

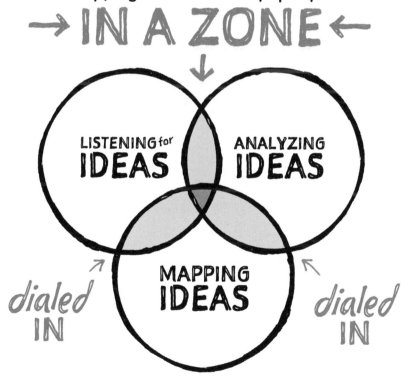

LISTENING for
IDEAS

ANALYZING
IDEAS

MAPPING
IDEAS

dialed
IN

dialed
IN

SKETCHNOTING TAPS *your* VISUAL LANGUAGE

A DETAILED DESCRIPTION VS. A SIMPLE DRAWING

A TREE is a woody perennial plant, typically having a single stem or trunk growing to a considerable height and bearing lateral branches at some distance from the ground.

Complex ideas can often be expressed more effectively as drawings.

Drawing an idea can often take just a fraction of the time needed to describe the same idea in verbal detail.

THE PYRAMIDS

THE SOLAR SYSTEM

ROCKY MOUNTAINS

KANSAS TORNADO

This is especially important when you're processing ideas in real time, and ideas are coming in fast.

SKETCHNOTING IS

Relaxing

o—+—o

WHEN I TOOK
PLAIN OL' NOTES,
I WAS ALWAYS

→ **WORRIED** ←

ABOUT MISSING
IMPORTANT DETAILS.

o—+—o

SWITCHING TO SKETCHNOTES

 *freed me*

TO FOCUS ON

LARGER THEMES
and IDEAS

I was able to relax, listen for key points, and capture those ideas *VISUALLY.*

Creating Sketchnotes is
DYNAMIC → and FUN!

The feeling I get from being completely connected while using my full verbal and visual thinking skills keeps me sketchnoting.

SKETCHNOTING allows you to relax, engage in the speaker's points, and have fun turning what's in your head into visual notes you'll want to share and refer to again and again.

RECAP

→ Dual coding theory suggests our brains process concepts in verbal and visual modes.

→ Using both modes creates cross-references, forming a visual map of what you capture.

→ Your visual map can help you recall details days, months, and even years later.

→ Sketchnoting improves your concentration because when you're engaged there's little room for distraction.

→ Practicing your sketchnoting technique again and again helps it feel more natural.

→ Sketchnoting can help you get into a zone.

→ Simple drawings can be quicker to create and more effective than detailed verbal descriptions.

→ Sketchnoting relaxes you; you let go of details in favor of large ideas.

★ NEXT: LISTEN UP!

MUJI

My favorite pens come from here

0.38 GEL INK PEN

"The cheap & cheerful standard "

ABCDE

HEX DOUBLE ENDED PEN

"Great for thick & thin marker lines "

ABC ABC

7 years as a developer and this cat never came out ...

JAVA IN A NUTSHELL

But then I met this polar bear ...

Information Architecture

(LIVE HERE)

LONDON

(GREW UP HERE)

MALAYSIA

(STUDIED HERE)

KANSAS

My name is **VERONICA ERB.**

I'm a UX Designer in Washington, DC.

@VERBISTHEWORD
VERONICAERB.COM

Hi!

STEP **1**

During the introduction.

PLAN.

Look for clues to give you an idea of what's coming.

TITTLE
🔑: the subject and structure of a talk. Fairly reliable.

DESCRIPTION
🔑: just the overall idea of a talk. Often unreliable due to speaker's polishing of talk.

SPEAKER STYLE
🔑: hints of structure & pacing.

(This 2-page spread had WAY more planning than any note should.)

STEP **2**

The majority of the talk!

CAPTURE.

First things first.

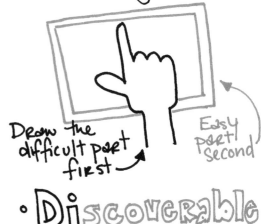

Draw the difficult part first

Easy part second

• **Discoverable**

Get the first two letters down quickly; add the rest when you have time.

I STARTED sketchnoting to practice committing ideas to paper. Because I had a visual vocabulary from years of drawing for FUN, I have focused on creating efficient and communicative notes. Now, I have a PROCESS:

STEP 3

Wrap up and Q&A.

REFINE.

connect ideas WITH ARROWS

fix mistakes WITH TEXTURE

add pizazz WITH FRAMES

TEXT

and CORRECT HIERARCHY WITH all three.

STEP 4

Whenever you get the chance!

TRY AGAIN.

Sketchnoting is a SKILL that you can improve each time you practice it. Give yourself enough space to...

LEARN FROM EACH NOTE YOU MAKE.

Good luck, and have FUN!
—V.

CHAPTER 3

LISTEN UP!

CAPTURING & CREATING SKETCHNOTES BEGINS WITH ACTIVE LISTENING SKILLS. AFTER ALL, IF YOU AREN'T HEARING IDEAS ACCURATELY, YOU CAN'T TURN THOSE IDEAS INTO EFFECTIVE SKETCHNOTES.

the KEYS to
LISTENING:

→ **FOCUS**
your attention on the speaker.

→ **ELIMINATE**
the distractions around you.

→ **IMMERSE**
yourself in the presentation.

When you're listening actively,

YOUR MIND can CACHE IDEAS and → SPOT PATTERNS.

ACTIVE LISTENING can help you synthesize and capture big ideas as sketchnotes.

··———··

MY LISTENING APPROACH

 ## DIRECT My Attention

By focusing on the speaker's words and the ideas being communicated, as well as reading the speaker's body language, I set aside other thoughts as I work.

 ## ELIMINATE and Filter Distractions

I'm proactive about eliminating the distractions I can and filtering out the distractions I can't eliminate. For example, I turn off alerts on my phone but must filter out noisy neighbors.

IMMERSE My Mind
IN THE Presentation

Giving my undivided attention and managing distractions allows me to concentrate completely on the message being shared. When I'm successful, I'm absorbed in the ideas I'm hearing and I'm able to synthesize them and process the information on paper.

 # CACHE Ideas

Through practice I've learned to hold an idea in my brain's cache area — a temporary space where I store thoughts while listening for the next idea. I sometimes use my cache and combine it with ideas I have on paper to help identify connections between ideas.

⊕ RECOGNIZE Patterns

When I'm listening actively, I can often pick up patterns in a speaker's presentation. Listening for patterns helps me illustrate those patterns in my sketchnotes, like these:

the 3 POINT SERMON

3 clear, logical steps — much like a sermon.

MEANDERING STORYTELLING

3 seemingly unrelated stories that connect at the end of a presentation.

PRACTICE your LISTENING SKILLS!

LISTENING SKILLS STRENGTHEN WITH USE.

Find opportunities to apply these listening techniques at meetings and conferences, and while watching video presentations online.

As you train your ears and mind, your ability to listen and to capture ideas will keep improving.

R E C A P

→ Capturing sketchnotes begins with hearing accurate information.

→ When you listen actively, your mind can spot patterns and cache ideas.

→ Give your undivided attention.

→ Eliminate and filter distractions.

→ Immerse your mind in the presentation.

→ Cache ideas.

→ Recognize patterns.

→ Practice to improve your listening skills at every opportunity.

⭐ **NEXT: THE SKETCHNOTING PROCESS**

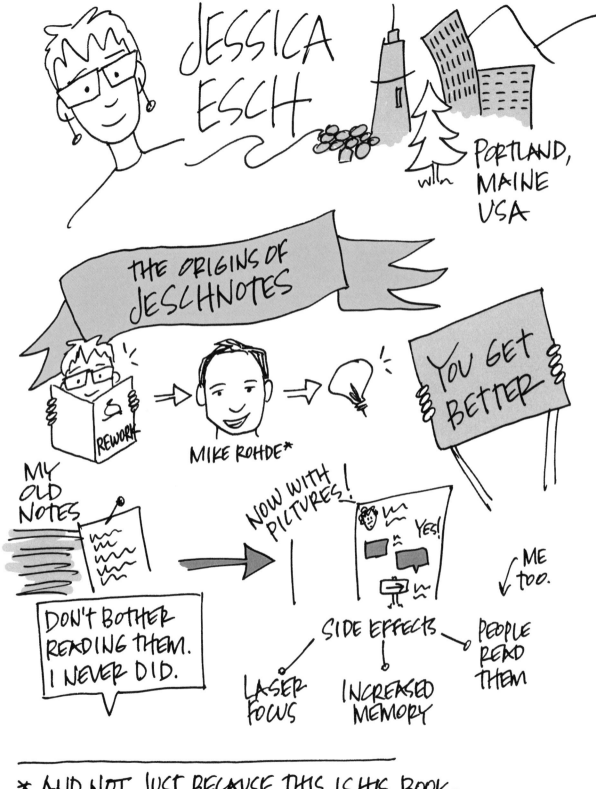

#JESCHENTIALS
JESCH ROMAN
MOLESKINE (3.5 x 5.5) GRID
UNIBALL VISION MICRO
I LOVE A THIN, BLACK LINE.
TALK BUBBLES
SMALLER PAGES SCARE ME LESS THAN BIG ONES
THE LIVE UNITED LIBRARY
United Way
LUbrary
UNITEDWAYGP.ORG
I CREATED MY OWN JOB HERE IN 2011
SAYITBEST.COM
flickr: JESCHNOTES
@JESCH30
RELAX
YOU WILL MISS MANY THINGS.
BE GENTLE WITH YOURSELF.
DON'T JUDGE TOO QUICKLY.
DYNOMITE
I COMPLETELY BLEW IT AT ONE TALK. IT WAS <<AWFUL>> BUT... I FILLED IN THE GAPS LATER AND NO ONE EVER KNEW.
EPIC FAILURE

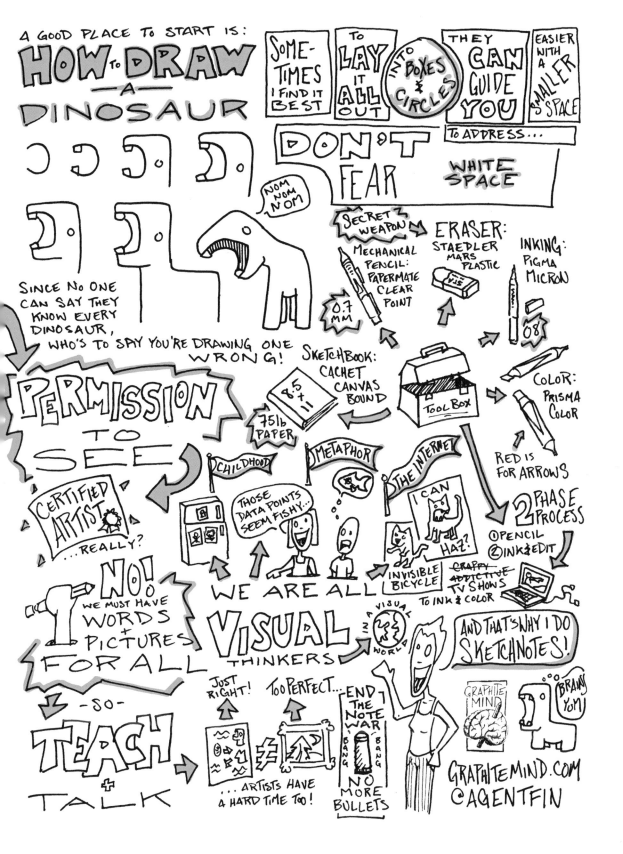

the Sketchnoting PROCESS

AFTER YEARS OF EXPERIENCE I'VE DEVELOPED MY OWN SKETCHNOTING PROCESS THAT WORKS WELL FOR ME AND CAN HELP YOU CREATE A PROCESS OF YOUR OWN.

HERE ARE THE STEPS I FOLLOW WHEN SKETCHNOTING EVENTS:

iPads are great tools for research before and at an event.

1 RESEARCH

Before I arrive onsite, I research the event, the speakers, and the topic.

RESEARCH GIVES ME INSIGHT and confidence, especially when I'm sketchnoting people or ideas that I'm new to.

Sometimes I'll bring my research along as printed pages as a backup in addition to my electronic research tools.

2 GATHER MATERIALS

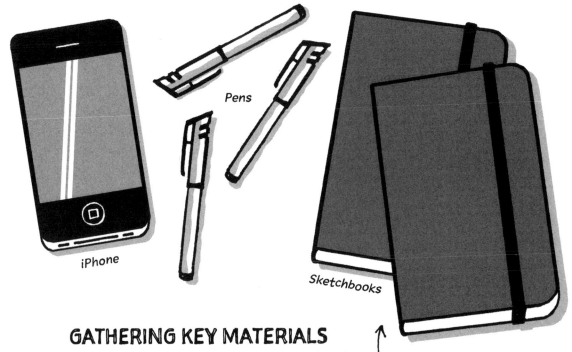

iPhone

Pens

Sketchbooks

GATHERING KEY MATERIALS

before arriving at an event is critical. I like to bring two or three Moleskine sketchbooks; multiple pens; and my iPhone to access photos and research materials, and to act as a flashlight in a pinch. A book light is useful if the venue is dark.

A few years ago, I was at an event in Chicago when my sketchbook literally came apart at the seams. Now I always carry at least one spare sketchbook, just in case.

ALWAYS BRING BACKUPS

You never know when a pen might run out of ink or a sketchbook might get damaged. Bring spares along to be safe.

Booklight

3 ARRIVE EARLY

I arrive at a presentation early and scout out the best seating. Spots underneath lights and close to the front allow me to hear and see the speaker.

SITTING IN THE MIDDLE OF A ROW can reduce annoyances or disruptions if others are coming in late or leaving early.

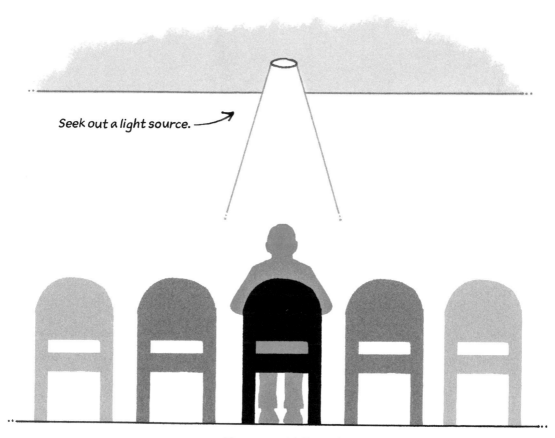

Seek out a light source.

Choose a middle seat.

4 CREATE A TITLE

A completed title page, ready to go.

I like to use my iPhone to find photos of the speaker for reference on my title page.

ONCE I'VE SETTLED IN, I check the topic and the speaker's name, verify spellings, and sometimes find a photo on my phone to create a visually interesting title page for the speaker or the topic.

••——————••

I complete my title before the speaker begins, so I can focus on the talk rather than rushing to create a title at the start of the presentation.

••——————••

 5 SKETCHNOTE

When the talk begins, I listen, synthesize the ideas I'm hearing, and start drawing what I'm thinking about as sketchnotes in my sketchbook.

 A completed sketchnote. →

6 PHOTOGRAPH

When I'm done sketchnoting, I shoot photos of my sketchnotes. This is a great way to immediately share what you've created via social media, and photos serve as a good backup of your sketchnotes.

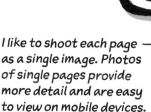 I like to shoot each page → as a single image. Photos of single pages provide more detail and are easy to view on mobile devices.

7 SCAN, TUNE & POST

When I get home, I scan my sketchnotes at high resolution, adjust the contrast, and fix any typos or errors in Photoshop. Final scans are exported to PNG formatted files for sharing online.

I use the same PNG files of my sketchnote scans to create a letter-sized, printable PDF document.

USB powered scanner

Sketchnotes scanned and assembled as a PDF document.

CONFERENCE ORGANIZERS

share sketchnotes to promote their upcoming events to potential attendees because they capture the event simply and visually.

Organizers often like to give away copies of the sketchnotes as PDF documents or printed booklets to their attendees. These after-event documents work well as handy offline references.

This printed booklet was created as a gift for the attendees of Summit Basecamp by the organizers. Booklets can also work great as a promotional item for the organizers.

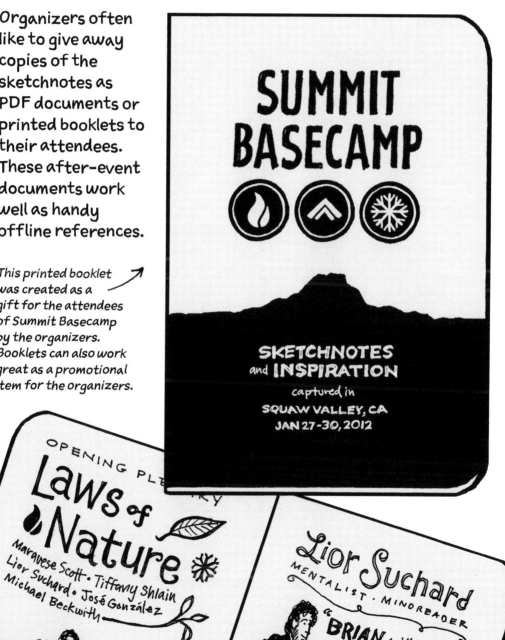

SUMMIT BASECAMP

SKETCHNOTES and INSPIRATION

captured in
SQUAW VALLEY, CA
JAN 27-30, 2012

OPENING PLENARY

Laws of Nature

Maravese Scott • Tiffany Shlain
Lior Suchard • José González
Michael Beckwith

Lior Suchard
MENTALIST • MINDREADER

"BRIAN will say 27"

"LIOR, PLEASE MEET DAN"

ANATOMY OF A SKETCHNOTE

I've created a map of sketchnote elements from an existing sketchnote so you can see and better understand each element.

★ TITLES

Titles are ideal for defining sketchnotes. They can include an event name, speaker names, date, location, and topic. Multiple talks at the same event can follow a consistent design for unity, or each speaker's title can be fun and unique.

TAKE TIME TO CREATE A TITLE BEFORE YOU BEGIN YOUR SKETCHNOTES.

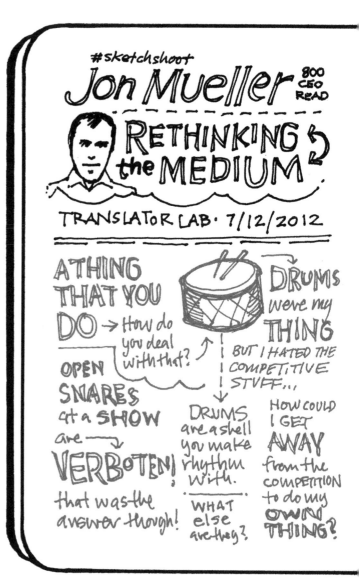

★TYPOGRAPHY

Typography is useful to emphasize ideas, create a hierarchy and structure, and even establish a mood.

★ DIAGRAMS & DRAWINGS

Diagrams and drawings make for more interesting elements.
A few pen strokes can illustrate complex ideas quickly.

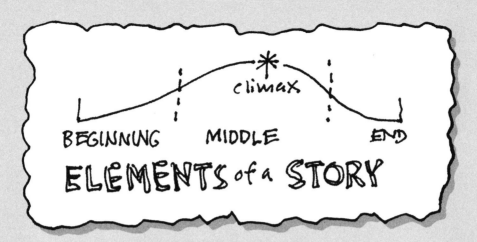

★ HANDWRITING
Handwriting is helpful for adding a detailed description if a diagram or information is needed.

IVON led the University of Alabama in the creation of an official Mobile app for the university.

★ DIVIDERS
Dividers like rules, dotted lines, and so on can help separate ideas from each other visually, creating order and structure.

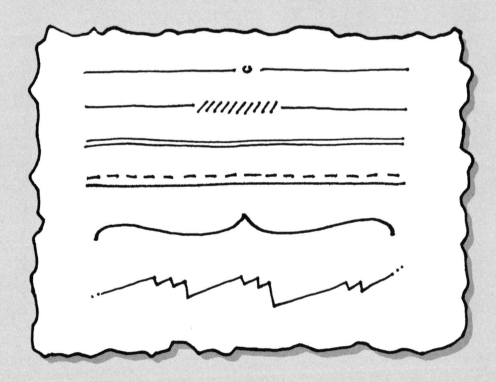

★ARROWS

Arrows point out details and can help focus attention on specific drawings, typography, or text, and they can provide a connection between multiple ideas.

★ BULLETS

Bullets are useful for identifying a series of ideas or highlighting a single idea among drawings or text. Different types of bullet icons can further define ideas.

★ ICONS

Icons are handy to use throughout a sketchnote document to identify ideas visually as repeating elements.

★ CONTAINERS

Containers connect various elements together in a single grouping to represent an overall idea or topic.

★ SIGNATURES

Signatures are an optional way to identify sketchnotes. If you're creating sketchnotes for your own use, no signature is required.

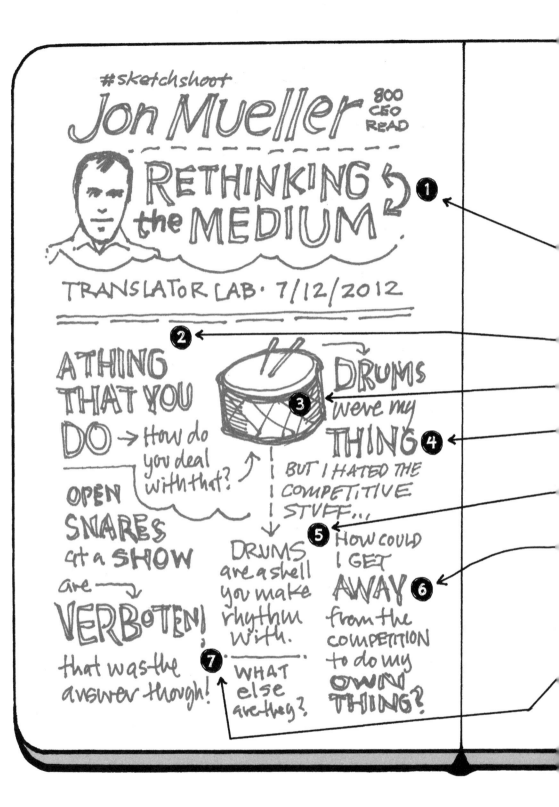

A SKETCHNOTE
from START to FINISH

To help you see the progression of a sketchnote from start to finish, I've labeled each section with a number and provided a brief descripton to show why and in which order each area was drawn.

1 The title creation was done before the event, using a photo of the speaker, Jon Mueller, on my iPhone.

2 For the first idea, I captured "A THING THAT YOU DO."

3 Jon talked about a snare drum, so my first drawing was of a drum.

4 Here I've fitted "DRUMS WERE MY THING" into this snug space on the right side of the snare drum drawing.

5 An arrow points to another idea lower on the page.

6 I added a "DO MY OWN THING" concept in the lower-right area.

7 Here I emphasized the idea of snare drums being verboten.

With this first page of sketchnotes, I've used a radial pattern to organize the talk information. I'll talk about sketchnote patterns in Chapter 5.

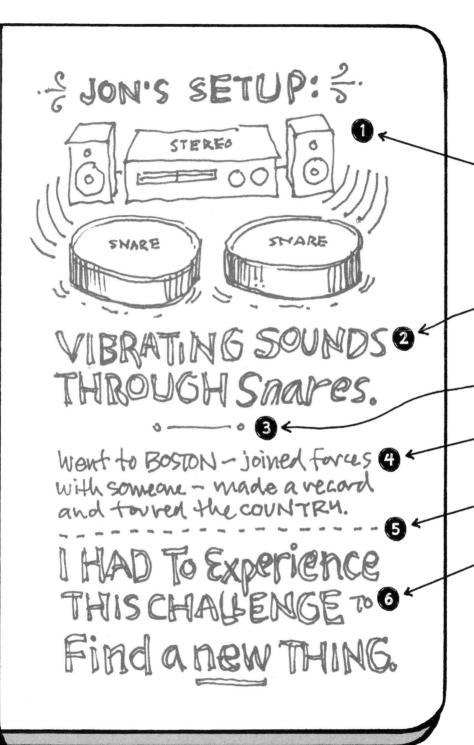

JON'S SETUP:

STEREO

SNARE   SNARE

VIBRATING SOUNDS ② THROUGH Snares.

○ ─── ○ ③

Went to BOSTON – joined forces ④ with someone – made a record and toured the COUNTRY.

------ ⑤

I HAD To Experience THIS CHALLENGE to ⑥ Find a new THING.

A SKETCHNOTE
from START to FINISH

1 Here I added a drawing of Jon's drum setup as I pictured it in my mind's eye. I added the title after drawing the image.

2 This description of Jon's approach to sending sounds through snare drums was key to the presentation, so I gave it focus with large, ALL CAPS typography.

3 I used a separator to create a break between the top and bottom.

4 Jon mentioned driving to Boston, creating a record, and touring the country, so I added it just below the separator.

5 Here's another separator using dashed lines.

6 To wrap up my sketchnotes, I used bold type to emphasize the speaker's final thought.

On the second page of my sketchnotes, I used a linear pattern for the information with heavier emphasis on drawings and typography.

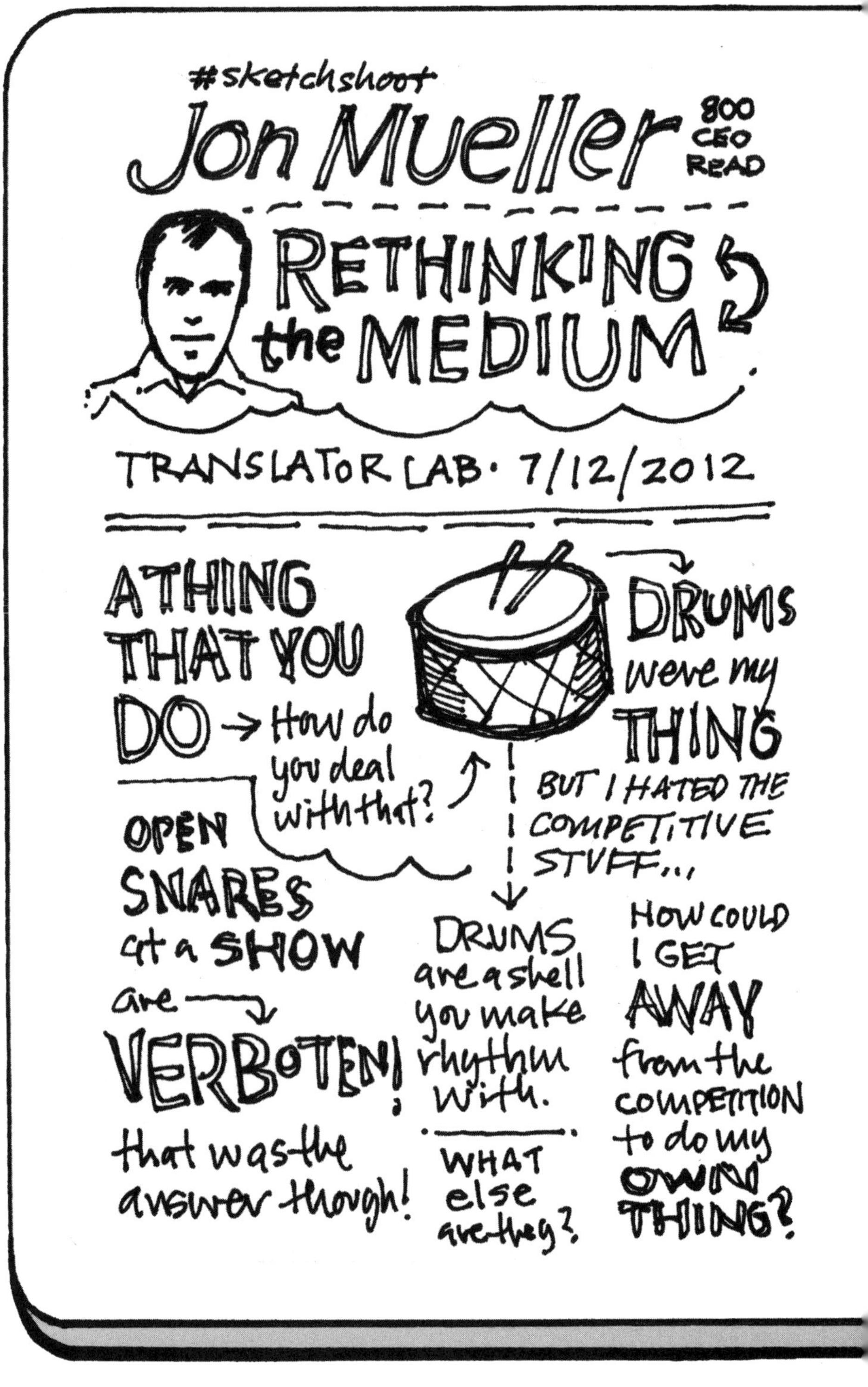

#sketchshoot

Jon Mueller 800 CEO READ

RETHINKING the MEDIUM

TRANSLATOR LAB · 7/12/2012

A THING THAT YOU DO → How do you deal with that?

DRUMS were my THING

BUT I HATED THE COMPETITIVE STUFF...

OPEN SNARES at a SHOW are → VERBOTEN!

that was the answer though!

DRUMS are a shell you make rhythm with.

WHAT else are they?

HOW COULD I GET AWAY from the COMPETITION to do my OWN THING?

JON'S SETUP:

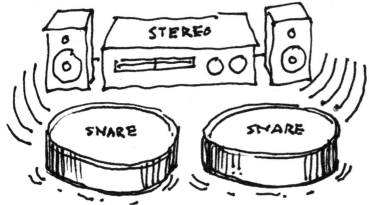

VIBRATING SOUNDS THROUGH Snares.

•———•

Went to BOSTON – joined forces with someone – made a record and toured the COUNTRY.

- - - - - - - - - - - - - - - - - - -

I HAD To Experience THIS CHALLENGE to Find a new THING.

DO YOUR RESEARCH

—and—

ARRIVE A BIT EARLY!

Being prepared helps you relax when the time comes to listen, cache ideas, and draw them.

RECAP

→ Use my process as a starting point, and then make it your own.

→ Research speakers and topics to gain insight and confidence.

→ Backups are key to being prepared when you're sketchnoting.

→ Arrive early, scout your location, and use the extra time to create a title *before* the event.

→ Photograph your sketchnotes right after the event to share them, and to have a backup.

→ Shared sketchnotes are great resources for attendees and work well as PR tools.

→ The anatomy of a sketchnote includes the title, typography, diagrams & drawings, handwriting, dividers, arrows, bullets, icons, containers, and signatures.

★ NEXT: TYPES OF SKETCHNOTES

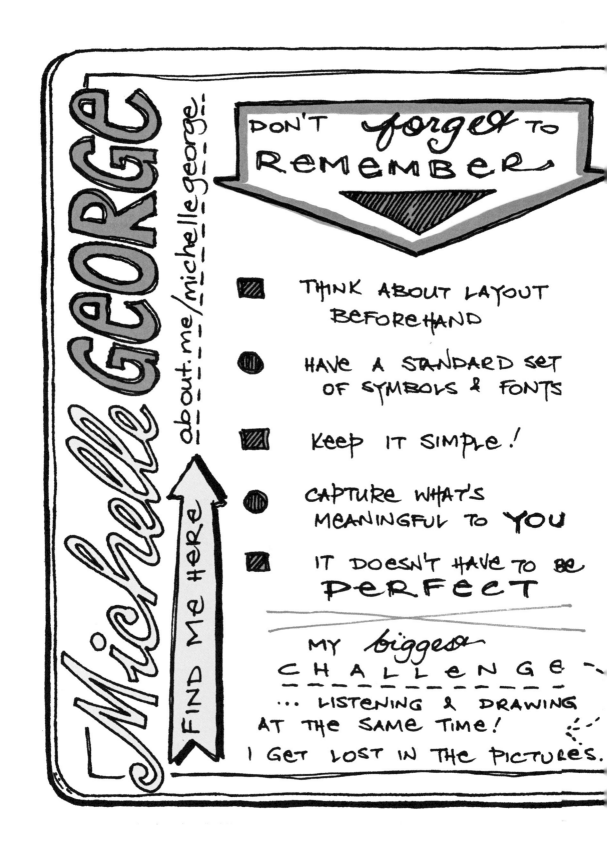

sketching ≠ drawing
sketchnotes = illustration

QUICK   EXPLORING IDEAS

PLANNED + LAYED OUT   DETAILED
FINISHED

IMPROVISED & playful

(this piece is more of an illustration)

develop your own
VISUAL VOCABULARY & STYLE

PLAY WITH SHAPES

SKETCH AN OBJECT 50 TIMES TO MAKE IT YOURS...

surprise yourself

PRO-PORT-IONS

CELEBRATE HAPPY ACCIDENTS

DIRECTION + DYNAMICS

CHAPTER 5

TYPES of Sketchnotes

SKETCHNOTES ARE A BLEND OF PERSONAL STYLE AND THE IDEAS YOU HEAR, ANALYZE, AND CAPTURE. LET'S LOOK AT BLENDING STYLE WITH THINKING, STRUCTURE, AND SKETCHNOTING PATTERNS.

STYLE PLUS THINKING

Sketchnotes are beautiful because of their variety and personality. Each sketchnote is created in a distinct, individual style, reflecting the person who creates it.

Sunni Brown • Getting Things Done

Jessica Esch • Rich Petersen

BUT MORE
than just style, sketchnotes reveal the thinking processes of their creator. Sketchnotes convey what the person is hearing, how that person analyzes and processes information, and what is most relevant in that person's view.

BY LOOKING AT SKETCHNOTES — THEIR STYLE AND STRUCTURE — I CAN BETTER UNDERSTAND HOW THEIR AUTHOR THINKS.

LET STYLE INSPIRE YOU

You may notice that many of the sketchnotes in this book are beautifully illustrated. Professional illustrators and designers, with years of visual experience, have created them.

Gerren Lamson • BbWorld 2012

IF YOU'RE NOT AN ARTIST, don't let these sketchnotes discourage you. Instead, look to them for inspiration and ideas, and keep in mind that you're just starting as a sketchnoter.

Whatever your skill level, be happy with where you are. Create sketchnotes and have fun, and work to improve your skills.

The ART & STRUCTURE SCALE

A helpful way to keep your current skills in perspective is to view sketchnotes that progress across a continuum:

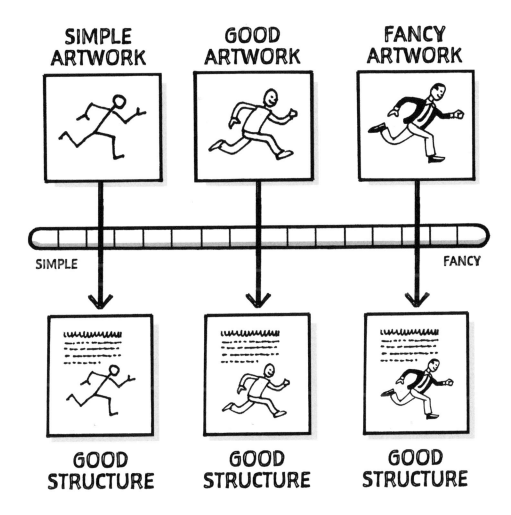

ALWAYS GOOD STRUCTURE REGARDLESS of ART QUALITY.

AT ONE END OF THE SCALE

you'll see ideas represented as rough drawings
by regular people. Even using simple drawings,
these sketchnotes use structure to capture
ideas effectively on the page.

AT THE OTHER END

you'll see beautiful illustrations created by experienced
professionals. Although the art may be more refined,
the key to a sketchnote is a logical organization that
makes sense and captures the ideas.

THINK OF
GOOD
STRUCTURE
as MEAT and
POTATOES,
AND FANCY ART as the
GRAVY ON TOP.

SKETCHNOTING PATTERNS

In the last five years I've reviewed many sketchnotes and have found that most fall into a few patterns:

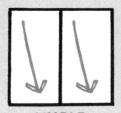

LINEAR

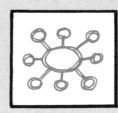

RADIAL

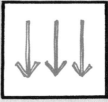

VERTICAL

PATH

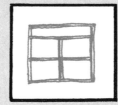

MODULAR

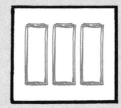

SKYSCRAPER

POPCORN

LINEAR

Following the pattern of a printed book, the linear sketchnote format shows information diagonally from the top left to the bottom right of a page or spread of two pages.

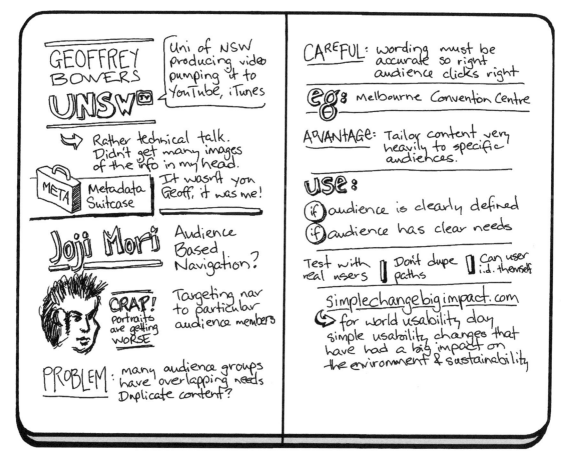

GEOFFREY BOWERS
UNSW📺 ← Uni of NSW producing video pumping it to YouTube, iTunes

⟳ Rather technical talk. Didn't get many images of the info in my head.

META Metadata Suitcase

It wasn't you Geoff, it was me!

Joji Mori — Audience Based Navigation?

CRAP! portraits are getting WORSE

Targeting nav to particular audience members

PROBLEM: many audience groups have overlapping needs Duplicate content?

CAREFUL: wording must be accurate so right audience clicks right

eg: Melbourne Convention Centre

ADVANTAGE: Tailor content very heavily to specific audiences.

USE:
(if) audience is clearly defined
(if) audience has clear needs

Test with real users ⏸ Don't dupe paths ⏸ Can user i.d. themself

simplechangebigimpact.com
↳ for world usability day simple usability changes that have had a big impact on the environment & sustainability

Matt Balara • Oz IA 2009

THE LINEAR PATTERN is what I typically use for my sketchnotes for two reasons: I like the story-like, linear flow of information on the page, and it works well in the two-page spreads I use in hardcover sketchbooks.

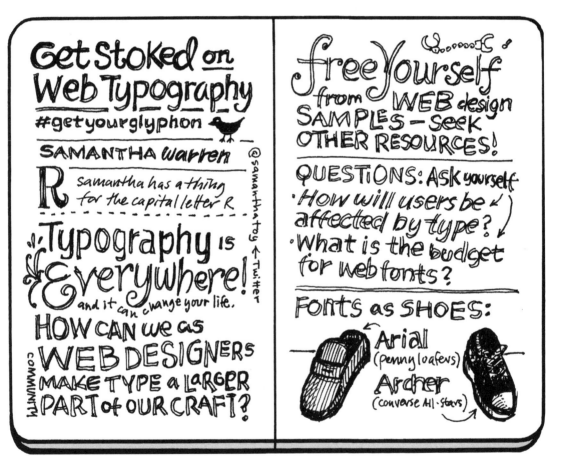

Get Stoked on Web Typography

#getyourglyphon

SAMANTHA Warren

@samanthatoy ← Twitter

R — samantha has a thing for the capital letter R

Typography is Everywhere! and it can change your life.

HOW CAN we as WEB DESIGNERS MAKE TYPE a LARGER PART of OUR CRAFT?

COMMUNITY

free Yourself from WEB design SAMPLES - Seek OTHER RESOURCES!

QUESTIONS: Ask yourself
- How will users be affected by type?
- What is the budget for web fonts?

FONTS as SHOES:
Arial (penny loafers)
Archer (converse All-Stars)

Mike Rohde • SXSW Interactive 2010

92

SKETCHNOTING in a linear pattern frees you to use as many pages as needed to capture ideas. It's also easy to read, because it follows standard book structure that's been used for hundreds of years.

JUST DON'T RUN OUT OF PAGES!

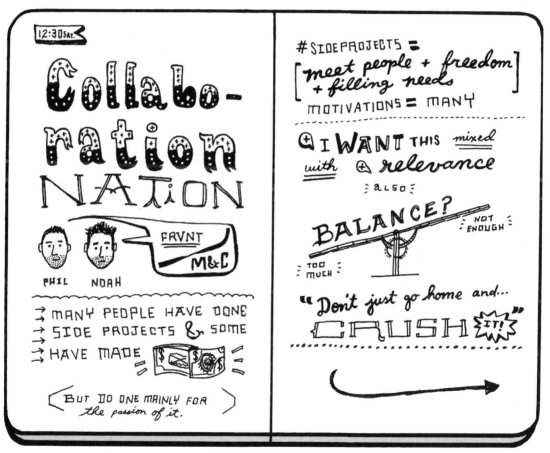

Gerren Lamson • SXSW Interactive 2011

HOWEVER, the rigid flow of linear sketchnotes can limit layout options, whereas the free-form radial sketchnote pattern, discussed next, provides more flexibility.

Carolyn Sewell • TypeCon 2011

RADIAL

The radial pattern roughly follows the structure of a bicycle wheel with the hub at the center and spokes radiating outward.

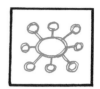

The center of a radial sketchnote may feature the name and drawing of the speaker or speakers who are presenting ideas, or the central topic.

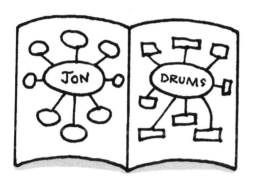

THE CENTRAL
HUB ESTABLISHES
THE OVERALL
CONCEPT, AND
IDEAS CREATE A
RADIATING PATTERN
MOVING OUTWARD
FROM THE CENTRAL HUB.

A RADIAL SKETCHNOTE doesn't have to be a perfect circle, and the hub doesn't need to be in the center of the page. This pattern can appear as an organic shape and still follow a hub-and-spoke structure.

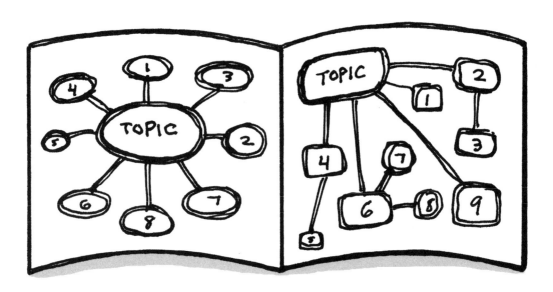

SYMMETRIC
CIRCULAR and
EQUALIZED

ASYMMETRIC
ORGANIC and
UNEQUAL

RADIAL
SKETCHNOTE

THIS RADIAL SKETCHNOTE FEATURES THE SPEAKER'S NAME AND TALK TITLE AT THE TOP-LEFT CORNER.

Eva-Lotta Lamm · Jessica Hische

THIS RADIAL SKETCHNOTE EMPHASIZES THE CONFERENCE NAME AT THE TOP OF THE PAGE.

Amanda Wright • dConstruct 2011

THE ADVANTAGE of a radial format is the freedom to add information wherever it fits in an outer spoke.

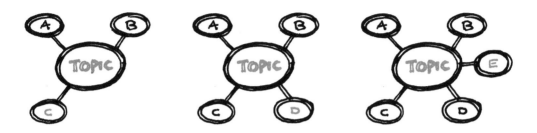

Because all of the spokes are connected to the central hub, clockwise, counterclockwise, or random patterns can work well with the radial sketchnote format.

Radial sketchnotes can sometimes make a reader work a bit harder to comprehend the pattern of ideas, because the information is structured in a complex, nonlinear way.

VERTICAL

Similar to a linear pattern, vertical sketchnotes present information in a single flow, from the top to the bottom of the page.

THIS PATTERN can be handy because it allows you to continue adding information vertically, as needed. The vertical pattern also provides a clear direction and structure for a reader to follow.

HOWEVER, LIKE THE LINEAR PATTERN, THE VERTICAL PATTERN CAN LIMIT LAYOUT OPTIONS AND CAN BE ONLY AS LONG AS THE VERTICAL HEIGHT OF YOUR PAPER OR DRAWING APP'S CANVAS.

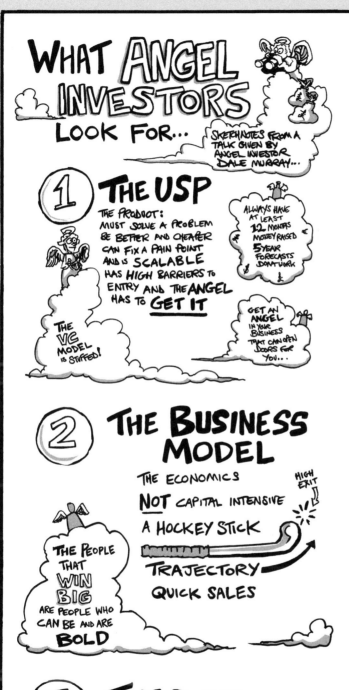

WHAT ANGEL INVESTORS LOOK FOR...

SKETCHNOTES FROM A TALK GIVEN BY ANGEL INVESTOR DALE MURRAY...

1 THE USP

THE PRODUCT:
MUST SOLVE A PROBLEM
BE BETTER AND CHEAPER
CAN FIX A PAIN POINT
AND IS SCALABLE
HAS *HIGH* BARRIERS TO
ENTRY AND THE ANGEL
HAS TO **GET IT**

ALWAYS HAVE
AT LEAST
12 MONTHS
MONEY RAISED
5 YEAR
FORECASTS DON'T WORK

THE VC MODEL IS STUFFED!

GET AN ANGEL IN YOUR BUSINESS THAT CAN OPEN DOORS FOR YOU...

2 THE BUSINESS MODEL

THE ECONOMICS
NOT CAPITAL INTENSIVE
A HOCKEY STICK
TRAJECTORY
QUICK SALES

HIGH EXIT

THE PEOPLE THAT **WIN BIG** ARE PEOPLE WHO CAN BE AND ARE **BOLD**

3 THE DEAL

NOT TO CLEAR A BALANCE SHEET
HAS TO BE SPENT TO
DEVELOP AN ASSET
ANGELS WANT **10** TIMES THEIR
MONEY BACK !!

WHAT ANGEL INVESTORS LOOK FOR...

SKETCHNOTES FROM A TALK GIVEN BY ANGEL INVESTOR DALE MURRAY...

1 THE USP
THE PRODUCT:
MUST SOLVE A PROBLEM
BE BETTER AND CHEAPER
CAN FIX A PAIN POINT
AND IS SCALABLE
HAS HIGH BARRIERS TO
ENTRY AND THE ANGEL
HAS TO **GET IT**

ALWAYS HAVE AT LEAST 12 MONTHS MONEY RAISED 5 YEAR FORECASTS DON'T WORK

THE VC MODEL IS STUFFED!

GET AN ANGEL IN YOUR BUSINESS THAT CAN OPEN DOORS FOR YOU...

2 THE BUSINESS MODEL
THE ECONOMICS
NOT CAPITAL INTENSIVE
A HOCKEY STICK
TRAJECTORY
QUICK SALES

HIGH EXIT

THE PEOPLE THAT **WIN BIG** ARE PEOPLE WHO CAN BE AND ARE **BOLD**

3 THE DEAL
NOT TO CLEAR A BALANCE SHEET
HAS TO BE SPENT TO
DEVELOP AN ASSET
ANGELS WANT 10 TIMES THEIR
MONEY BACK !!
ANGEL INVESTING IS RISKY 1 OUT OF 10 SUCCESSFUL
EVERYONE HAS TO
GET RICH!

THERE ARE OPEN 4-5 ANGELS TO FUNDING

YOU COULD WRITE A BOOK ON FINGER IN THE AIR VALUATIONS!

4 THE PEOPLE
ULTRA-AMBITIOUS OVER ACHIEVERS
GETTING UP AT 4.30AM FOR TRAINING
A STRONG LEADER WHO COMMANDS
THE RESPECT OF THEIR STAFF
IT'S AN 8 TO 10 YEAR RELATIONSHIP
SO THE INVESTOR AND ENTREPRENEUR
BETTER GET ON!!

I HAVE 5 LIKE YOU

I LIKE THE CUT OF HIS JIB

TOP TIPS
- UNDERSTAND YOUR PRODUCT
- CONVEY YOUR PASSION
- MAKE A GOOD DEAL
- **BE NICE**

SKETCHNOTES BY CHRIS SHIPTON

Chris Shipton • Angel Investors

PATH

The path sketchnote pattern creates a path of information across the page vertically, horizontally, or diagonally. The path pattern can appear as a zigzag, c-shape, w-shape, or any organic path shape you can imagine.

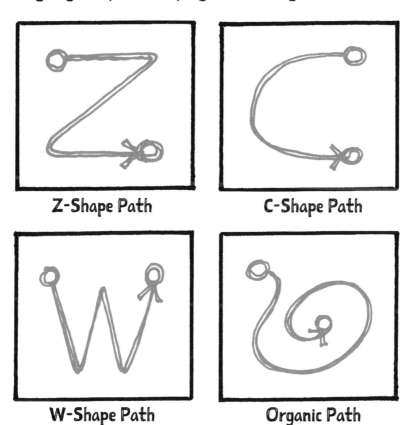

Z-Shape Path

C-Shape Path

W-Shape Path

Organic Path

USING A PATH PATTERN can be perfect for telling about an event or thought process using a series of steps that work well when following an organic shape.

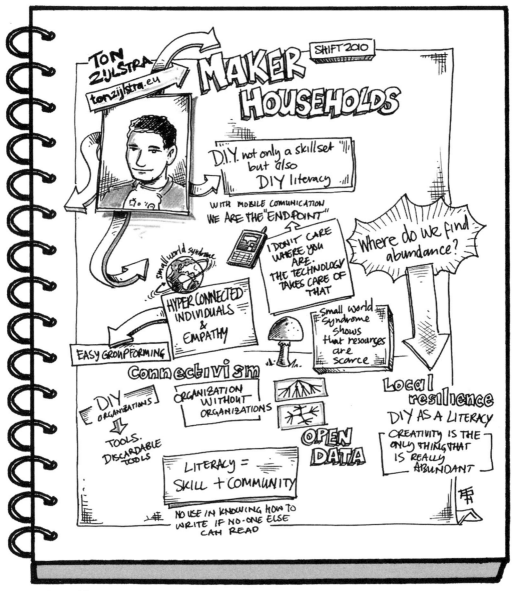

Bauke Schildt • Ton Zijlstra

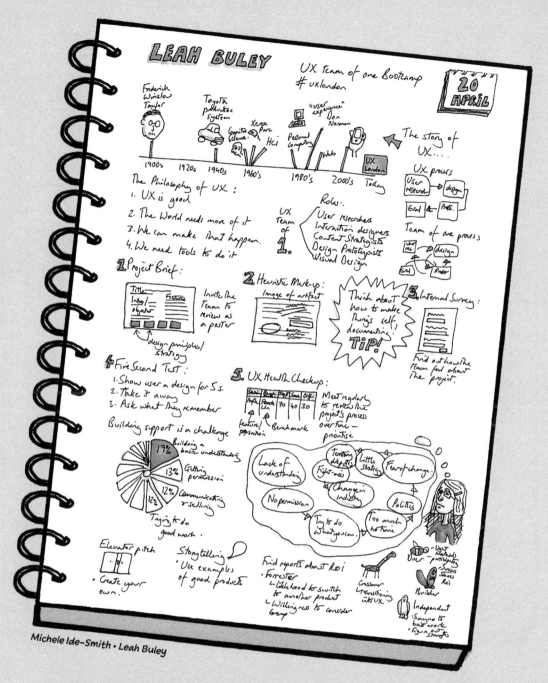

Michele Ide-Smith • Leah Buley

PATH PATTERNS do require a little planning, and if the information you're sketchnoting is more extensive than you've planned for, you may run out of room.

MODULAR

The modular pattern divides a single page or spread of pages into distinct regions or modules. Each module holds separate bits of information or different speakers within a larger event.

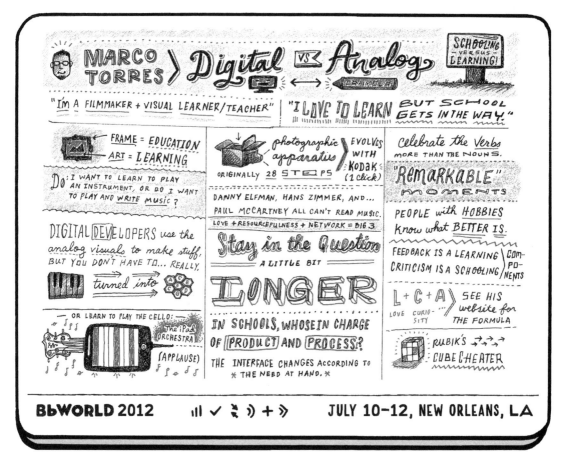

Gerren Lamson • BbWorld 2012

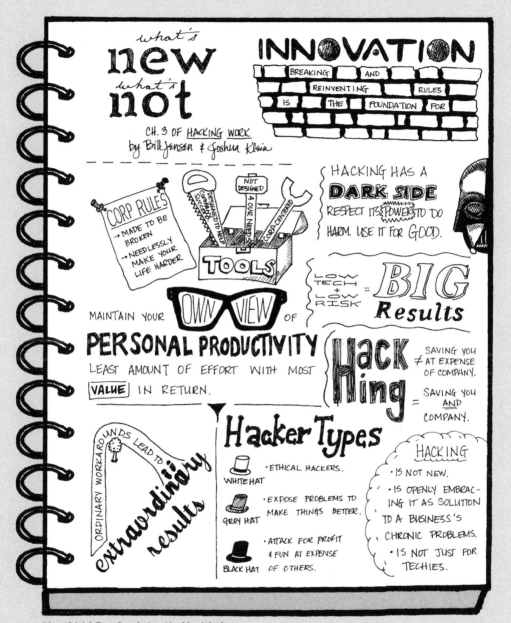

what's
new
what's
not

CH. 3 OF HACKING WORK
by Bill Jensen & Joshua Klein

INNOVATION

BREAKING AND REINVENTING RULES IS THE FOUNDATION FOR

CORP RULES
→ MADE TO BE BROKEN
→ NEEDLESSLY MAKE YOUR LIFE HARDER

NOT DESIGNED 4 OUR NEEDS

DESIGNED TO HELP COMPANIES SUCCEED

CORP-CENTERED

TOOLS

HACKING HAS A
DARK SIDE
RESPECT ITS POWER TO DO HARM. USE IT FOR GOOD.

LOW TECH + LOW RISK = **BIG** *Results*

MAINTAIN YOUR OWN VIEW OF

PERSONAL PRODUCTIVITY
LEAST AMOUNT OF EFFORT WITH MOST VALUE IN RETURN.

Hack Hing
SAVING YOU ≠ AT EXPENSE OF COMPANY.

= SAVING YOU AND COMPANY.

ORDINARY WORKAROUNDS LEAD TO *extraordinary results*

Hacker Types

WHITE HAT • ETHICAL HACKERS.

GREY HAT • EXPOSE PROBLEMS TO MAKE THINGS BETTER.

BLACK HAT • ATTACK FOR PROFIT & FUN AT EXPENSE OF OTHERS.

HACKING
• IS NOT NEW.
• IS OPENLY EMBRACING IT AS SOLUTION TO A BUSINESS'S CHRONIC PROBLEMS.
• IS NOT JUST FOR TECHIES.

Marichiel & Dan Boudwin • Hacking Work

A MODULAR PATTERN can work well if your goal is to organize information in a grid-like pattern or if you have many presentations to capture in a limited area.

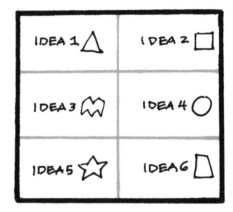

HOWEVER, USING MODULAR PATTERNS CAN LIMIT THE AMOUNT OF INFORMATION YOU CAN SKETCHNOTE, PARTICULARLY IF YOU'RE CAPTURING SEVERAL TALKS WITHIN A SINGLE MODULAR STRUCTURE.

Avoid running out of room with a modular sketchnote by establishing the module spaces before you begin. You can base them on the number of speakers or topics being covered at the event.

SKYSCRAPER

The skyscraper pattern is similar to the modular approach but divides the page into a series of tall, vertical panels, which contain separate bits of information.

This pattern can work great for panel discussions where multiple people are speaking at different times.

TO CREATE A SKYSCRAPER SKETCHNOTE,

use a vertical column for each speaker and add the person's name or portrait. When the panel discussion begins, simply add each person's comments into the appropriate column.

I. Names & Faces

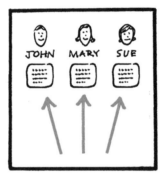

2. Capture comments

3. Fill out the page

MANAGING A SKYSCRAPER SKETCHNOTE

Remember to pace yourself with the limited space of a skyscraper sketchnote. Focus on the key phrases and words that are meaningful. Work on boiling down the idea you're hearing to its purest essence.

SKYSCRAPER SKETCHNOTES, LIKE OTHER TIGHTLY STRUCTURED PATTERNS, HAVE THE DISADVANTAGE OF LIMITED SPACE, REQUIRING MORE SELECTIVE QUOTE CAPTURE.

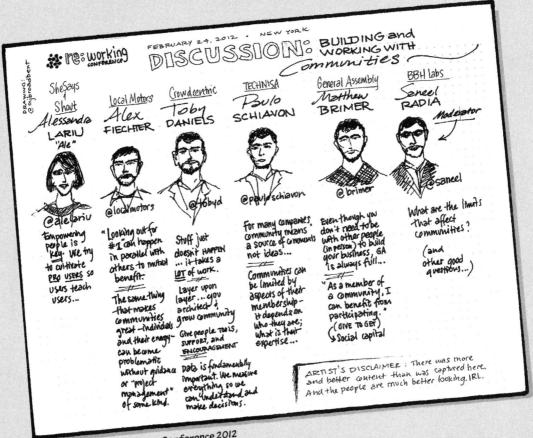

MJ Broadbent • Re:Working Conference 2012

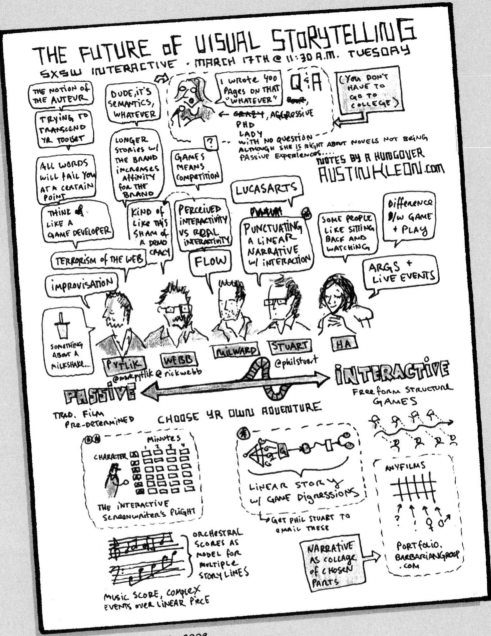

Austin Kleon • SXSW Interactive 2009

POPCORN

The popcorn pattern has the flexibility of placing information you're capturing in a free, random pattern. The topic, speaker name, and information tidbits can appear anywhere on the page.

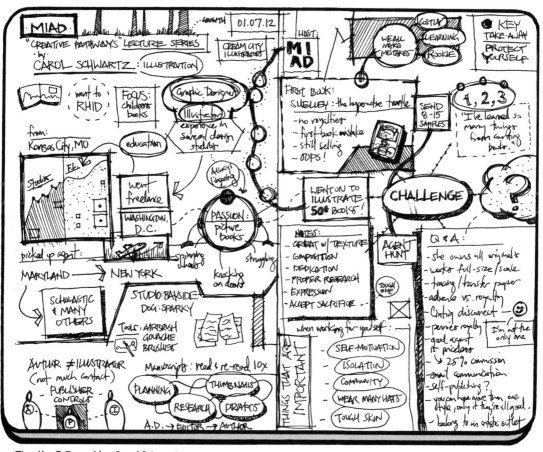

Timothy J. Reynolds • Carol Schwartz

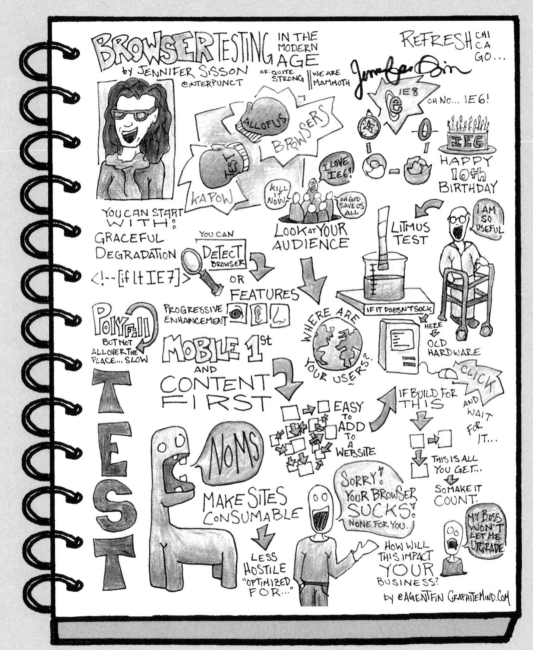

Alexis Finch • Jennifer Sisson

WITH THE POPCORN PATTERN, there is more emphasis on capturing information and less emphasis on placing it in a specific location. This approach can focus your mind on seizing ideas without worrying so much about their placement.

HOWEVER, THE RANDOM ARRANGEMENT OF THE FREE-FORM POPCORN PATTERN CAN MAKE YOUR SKETCHNOTE MORE DIFFICULT TO FOLLOW BECAUSE OF THE HAPHAZARD PLACEMENT OF INFORMATION.

PATTERNS ARE STARTING POINTS

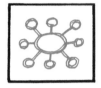

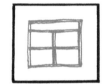

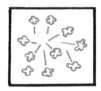

The patterns I've described are just some of
the main ways you can structure your sketchnotes.
These seven are starting points to help
kick-start your sketchnoting skills.

••—————————••

TRY OUT EACH PATTERN TO FIND
YOUR FAVORITES AND TO SUIT PARTICULAR
SITUATIONS. EXPERIMENT, MIX, MATCH,
AND DEVELOP YOUR OWN PATTERNS.

RECAP

→ Sketchnotes blend style and thinking, expressing the creator's personality.

→ If you're not an artist, use professionally illustrated sketchnotes as a model to inspire your own sketchnotes.

→ Always sketchnote with good structure regardless of your artistic skills.

→ Even if you're just starting to draw, you can make great sketchnotes with simple drawings and a good framework.

→ The seven common sketchnoting patterns are Linear, Radial, Vertical, Path, Modular, Skyscraper, and Popcorn.

→ Each pattern has benefits and drawbacks. Try each one to learn how different patterns work in different situations.

★ NEXT: SKETCHNOTING APPROACHES, HIERARCHY, AND PERSONALIZATION

Austin Kleon said
Draw the Talks...
OK!!
Here's a few Tips
Gerren Lamson
Follow the Most Inspiring Words
&
It's the right thing to do.
WWW.GERRENLAMSON.COM
Design and Illustration
Watch
"Be Quiet"
Shhh..
Listen & Draw..

MATTHEW MAGAIN

I DREW A LOT AS A KID, BUT BECAME A SOFTWARE ENGINEER AND IGNORED MY VISUAL MUSCLES FOR A FEW YEARS.

Freelance UX Designer

MELBOURNE AUSTRALIA

I LEFT A LARGE CONSULTING COMPANY BEFORE IT ERODED ♥ MY SOUL. ♥

TRAVEL REIGNITED MY PASSION FOR DESIGN & VISUAL THINKING

HACKEY SACK

TIPS

MASTER SKETCHING COMMON WORDS USED IN PRESENTATIONS.

CLOUD
SHIP
ZOOM
MAPS
IPHONE
TABLET

WANKEL ROTARY ENGINE — NOT ALL THAT COMMON BUT IT SOUNDS FUNNY!

PRACTICE BY WATCHING RECORDINGS

TED.com
UX WEEK.com
coursera.org

AIM FOR CURATION NOT COMPLETENESS

1.
2.
3.

FOCUS ON WHAT RESONATES WITH YOU.

YOU'RE CREATING A MEMENTO NOT A REFERENCE

MICHAEL, FROM **Microsoft** SAW MY SKETCHNOTES, AND HE ASKED ME TO **LIVE-SKETCHNOTE** THE REMIX 2011 KEYNOTE ON A **1m × 1m** CANVAS

I ALSO WROTE & ILLUSTRATED A CHILDREN'S BOOK ABOUT A MATHEMATICIAN WHO ATTEMPTS SOLO FLIGHT ☞ CHARLIEWEATHERBURN.COM

← PLUG

IN FRONT OF **500 PEOPLE**

IT WAS PRETTY AWESOME!

LILY SERNA

A GAME SHOW HOSTESS READ **A PAGE** OUT ON NATIONAL

TV!

BE A **C.R.A.P.** SKETCHER

CONTRAST

ie. make stuff really different

ALIGN-MENT

PROXIMITY

REPETITION
❀ flower
❀ another one
❀ look-another!

CHECK OUT THE NON-DESIGNER'S DESIGN BOOK.

WATCH THE CLOCK

IF THE TALK IS **HALFWAY DONE** AND YOU HAVEN'T FILLED HALF THE PAGE, *SPEED UP!*

MAKE USE OF

TYPE EMPATHY
e.g.
THOUGHTFUL

HEAVY

FLASHY

QUIET.

EPIC NERVOUS

LOUD

SAY HELLO!

🐦 mattymcg
ON THE WEB:
UXmastery.com

CHAPTER 6

SKETCHNOTING
APPROACHES,
HIERARCHY,
&personalization

WAYS TO SKETCHNOTE,
STRUCTURE YOUR WORK,
AND MAKE IT YOUR OWN.

THERE ARE TWO DIFFERENT APPROACHES TO CAPTURING SKETCHNOTES

REAL-TIME
SKETCHNOTES

TWO-STAGE
SKETCHNOTES

BOTH APPROACHES
emphasize the use of visual elements
and stress the importance of baking
personality into your sketchnotes.

REAL-TIME SKETCHNOTING

I, and many other sketchnoters, create sketchnotes live and in real time. When I'm working in the moment, I'm focused, tuned into the speaker, listening for big ideas, and synthesizing and converting what I'm hearing into visual notes.

SKETCHNOTING LIVE IS LIKE TAKING NOTES TRADITIONALLY, EXCEPT YOU'RE ADDING A WHOLE TOOLBOX OF VISUAL ELEMENTS TO YOUR NOTES, LIKE THESE:

- TYPOGRAPHY
- DRAWINGS
- HANDWRITING
- DIAGRAMS
- DIVIDERS
- ARROWS
- BULLETS
- ICONS
- CONTAINERS

Working in real time means you're listening for big ideas as you work.

KEEP

REAL-TIME SKETCHNOTING is not as hard as it may sound. It does mean you must be fully engaged in the presentation to decide what key information is worth capturing and what isn't.

TOSS

LIVE SKETCHNOTING IS A PRACTICE THAT IMPROVES WITH REPETITION. THE MORE YOU DO IT, THE BETTER YOUR LISTENING SKILLS, PATTERN RECOGNITION, AND DRAWING SKILLS WILL GET.

THE BIGGEST BENEFIT
OF LIVE SKETCHNOTING:

when THE event
IS DONE,
YOU
ARE
DONE.

TWO-STAGE SKETCHNOTING

Some sketchnoters use the second approach and create their notes in two stages — capturing rough sketchnotes first and then enhancing or re-creating them at a later time.

A TWO-STAGE, PENCIL TO INK APPROACH

This first variation of the two-stage approach to sketchnoting begins with real-time sketchnotes captured in pencil instead of ink.

At a later time, the sketchnoter inks over the original pencil lines, fine-tuning them and adding detail. This is a good time to add color with markers, pencil, or paint.

WITH THE PENCIL TO INK APPROACH,
you're working through your ideas twice, which means
they are reinforced in your memory.

You're still capturing notes in real time, but you have
the additional task of inking every pencil line again to
complete your sketchnotes.

..———————..

PENCILING SKETCHNOTES MAY LET YOU CORRECT ERRORS, BUT IT CAN ALSO TAKE TWICE AS MUCH TIME AS CREATING REAL-TIME, INKED SKETCHNOTES.

Oops!

Fixed.

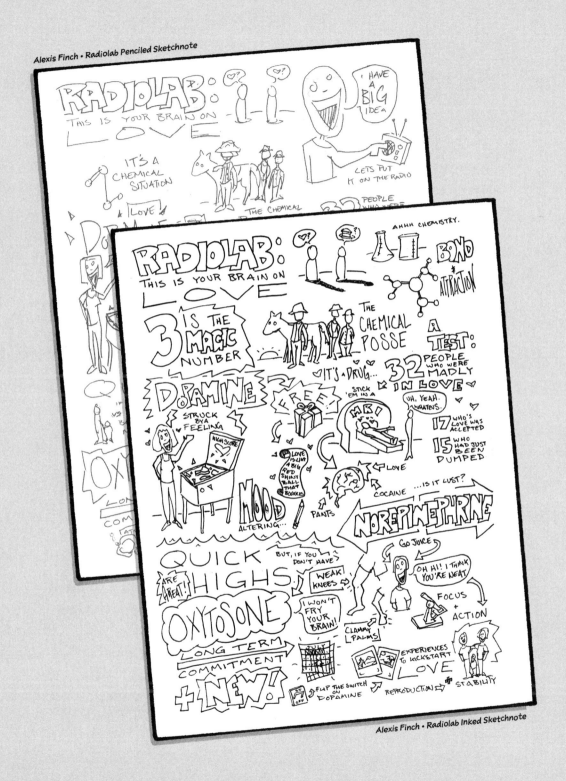

Alexis Finch • Radiolab Inked Sketchnote

B TWO-STAGE, ROUGH TO REFINED APPROACH

A second variation of the two-stage sketchnoting approach uses rough notes of text and visual elements, which are redrawn as final sketchnotes at a later time.

This approach puts less emphasis on making perfect sketchnotes on the spot. For some, this may be a good way to ease into sketchnoting.

YOU ARE PROCESSING NOTES TWICE, which may help your comprehension. However, like the pencil to ink method, this approach will likely take twice as much time as creating real-time, inked sketchnotes.

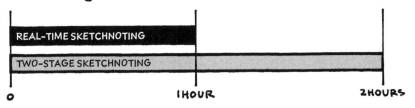

Rough Notes

Redrawn Notes

IT'S OK TO EXPERIMENT with two-stage sketchnoting if you're concerned about mistakes or you want to explore sketchnoting at a slower pace. But don't get stuck there. Real-time sketchnoting with ink is easier than you may think.

★

HOWEVER YOU
CREATE SKETCHNOTES,

remember:

·· · ··————————————————·· · ··

IT'S AN ACTIVE PRACTICE

·· · ··————————————————·· · ··

SKETCHNOTING
IS SOMETHING
YOU DO.

★

CREATING A HIERARCHY

When you create sketchnotes, one of your key tasks is to construct a logical hierarchy of information. Defining a hierarchy helps you, and others reading your sketchnotes, to understand the importance of the information you've captured.

HIERARCHY CREATES FLOW →

SPEAKER NAME and topic name set the overall context.

HEADLINES describe the broad subtopics.

SUBHEADS add detail to the headline's meaning.

DESCRIPTIVE TEXT adds more detail.

BULLET POINTS separate and define detail.

Speaker Name
THE TALK TOPIC

HEADLINE
The Subhead
Descriptive text is at the next level in the hierarchy

★ Bullet points are
★ Sub items under
★ The descriptive text

FLOW

HIERARCHY IN ACTION:

I use a variety of elements to indicate which bits of information are key points in a sketchnote hierarchy.

The top level in the hierarchy is the speaker's name and title.

Descriptive text establishes the talk.

The drawing of a couch emphasizes point no. 1.

Numbering of the points offers a clear hierarchy.

Andy Stanley

LEADERSHIP Confessions:

I may be in charge:
- but I don't have all the answers!

I'm not the smartest one in here - I'm just the LEADER.

LEADERS are IMPORTANT BECAUSE of UNCERTAINTy

THREE QUESTIONS:

1. WHAT would my replacement DO?

← An old couch w/ emotional attachment is fine in your house - but emotional attachments to old things can be dangerous in business.

*THINK as though YOU ARE THE PERSON replacing YOU.

2. WHAT would a GREAT LEADER DO?
→ A selfless, focused and passionate decision-maker

"IF WE GET better CUSTOMERS WILL demand WE GET BIGGER."
- TRUETT CATHY

Mike Rohde · Andy Stanley

A main point is captured as a quote using larger type.

An asterisk provides emphasis to the detail under item no. 1.

An arrow provides contrasting emphasis to the detail under item no. 2.

ELEMENTS OF HIERARCHY

To help guide the reader's eye through the flow of your sketchnotes, here are some handy elements you can use to emphasize hierarchy.

Bold Type

Bold type helps draw the eye to important ideas.

ALL CAPS

Using ALL CAPS is another way to bring attention to important ideas.

1. The First Concept
2. The Second Concept
   a. First sub item
   b. Second sub item

Numbers work well for providing a more structured hierarchy.

✳ ✳ → ★ ● ▲ ! ?

Icons are great for marking key ideas on their own or in bulleted lists.

PERSONALIZATION

Sketchnotes are personal. When you're hearing and processing ideas, your opinion naturally comes into play.

Your personality determines the decisions you make about which ideas to capture and what those ideas mean to you.

IN SIGN LANGUAGE INTERPRETING, the interpreter is charged with staying neutral, passing along *exactly* what is said by the speaker — nothing more and nothing less.

Sketchnotes don't have to be neutral. In fact, personal opinions expressed and embedded in sketchnotes are intriguing, because they reveal what the sketchnoter was hearing and thinking during the creation process.

PERSONALIZATION TIPS

Here are a few ideas for injecting your personality
into the sketchnotes you create:

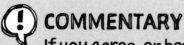 **COMMENTARY**
If you agree, or better yet, if you disagree
with an idea, capture your thoughts.

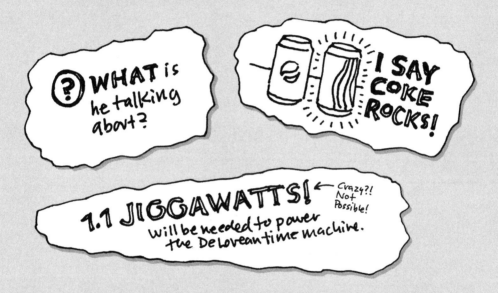

*Opinions embedded in your
sketchnotes can become a handy
reference for remembering those
thoughts later on.*

☺ HUMOR

If you find something that you hear funny, share your thoughts in context with the idea. Include humorous people, cartoon characters, or objects along with your humorous comments. Have fun!

& WHIMSY

Experiment with the style of type and elements you use as you sketchnote. You might use flourished script text and unusually shaped containers or icons; play with graphical elements like swirls, lines, or stars to emphasize ideas.

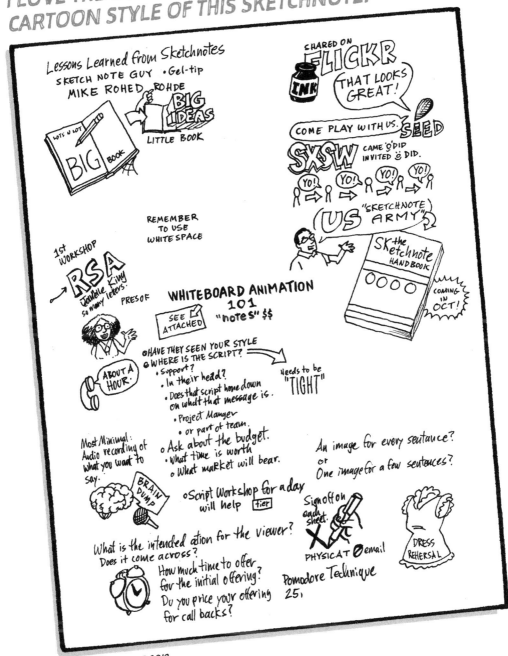

Mark Monlux • IFVP 2012

how to PENNY FARTHINGTON
DOUG MARCH @MARCHDOE 1/12/12

OHIO

Doug went to the UNIV. of DAYTON but he wasn't able to climb to the NBA-

inspired by Maggie's drawing

A BIT of HISTORY: 2 BROTHERS who did some amazing things & had some AWESOME ★ FASHION SENSE = the WRIGHT BROTHERS perhaps the first hipsters

ee "I SUCKED AT MATH & SCIENCE therefore ← NO ENGINEER

ee "IF I ASKED PEOPLE WHAT THEY WANTED, THEY WOULD HAVE ASKED FOR FASTER HORSES"
henry ford

REITERATE / REITERATE / REITERATE

Erin M. Hawkins • Doug March

SXSW
South x South West
AUSTIN Texas
INTERACTIVE FESTIVAL 2008
A SERIES of TOOLS:
WEB
SMS ★ TWITTER
MAIL ✉ VOICE ⊲))

Mike Rohde • SXSW Interactive 2008

RECAP

→ Real-time sketchnoting focuses on capturing the big, relevant ideas you hear.

→ Two-stage sketchnoting combines notes that are captured in a rough form first, and are either refined or re-created later on.

→ Sketchnoting is founded on traditional note taking, but adds more detail through type, drawings, and other visual elements.

→ Practice and repetition improve your real-time sketchnoting skills.

→ Use hierarchy and personalization to make sketchnotes unique and interesting.

→ Sketchnotes don't have to be neutral. Opinion, humor, and whimsy are great ways to personalize your sketchnotes.

★ NEXT: SKETCHNOTING SKILLS AND TECHNIQUES

TIMOTHY J. REYNOLDS

3D ILLUSTRATOR

CURRENTLY LIVING IN — MILWAUKEE, WISCONSIN

LAND OF BEER & CHEESE!

HI, I'M TIM.

favorite sketchbook:
Moleskine 'sketch' (large)

favorite pencil:
PRISMACOLOR blue indigo 'verithin'

favorite pen:
UNIBALL vision exact

PROCESS:

(see following PAGE)

I've been drawing since I was a kid. I carry my moleskine with me everywhere. I've always doodled during school, class, work, etc but I just never made any cohesive notes until a few years ago.

ENTER: obsession with taking sketchnotes. Now I look for reasons to go to any mundane meeting at work just to practice taking them.

WEBSITE

TURNISLEFTHOME.COM

LISTEN

1 The process always begins by listening, whether the speaker is live in front of you, or watching a video of a presentation. TED talks are great practice.

CAPTURE

2 Draw/sketch/write as fast as possible. Quick and loose gestures to capture the true bulk of the message. Get ready for a sore wrist afterwards. Don't worry, it's worth it.

CONNECT

3 Start connecting ideas by using arrows and dotted lines. Try and tie up loose notes with more similar messages. Making connections.

FINALIZE

4 Usually post-talk and I can finally relax a bit on my pace. I start adding shading, boxes, circles, along with more dots and shapes to help finalize the spread. Crosshatching is your friend.

[LAST, BUT NOT LEAST : SHARE]

TWITTER

@TURNISLEFTHOME

[ALSO SEE:] DRIBBBLE.COM/TURNISLEFTHOME (3D WORK!)
(Yes, 3 B's!)

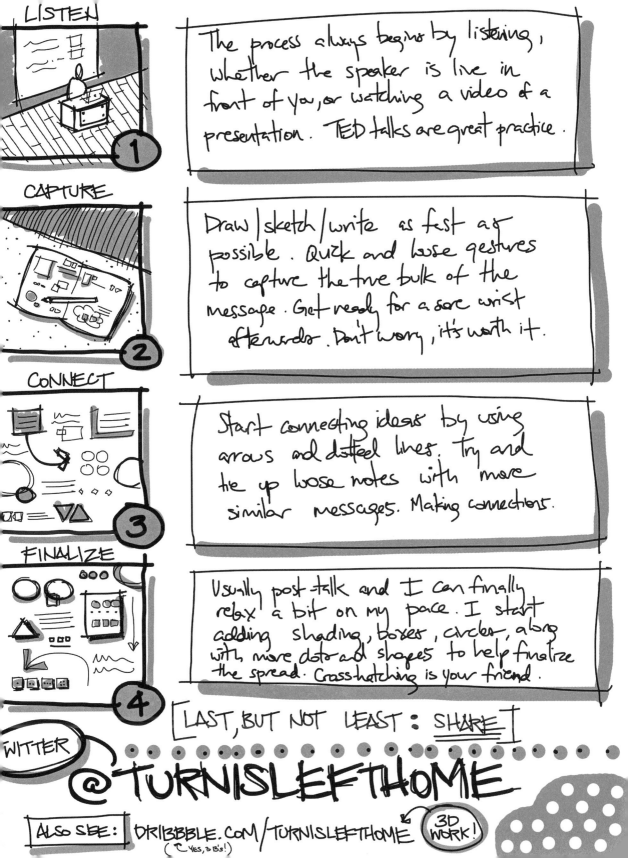

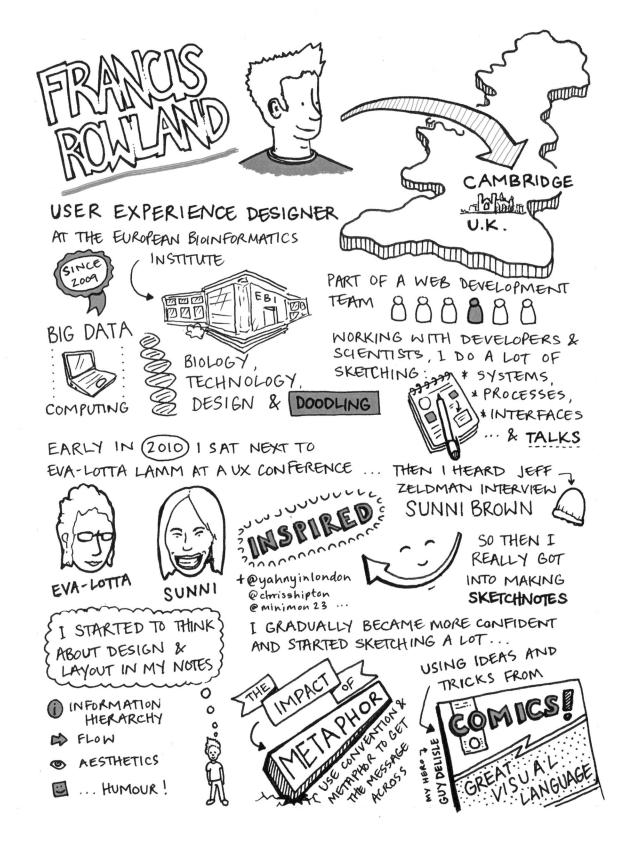

SO I SEEM TO HAVE DEVELOPED A **STYLE**

SOMETIMES OF COURSE, IT CAN BE HARD TO THINK OF WHAT TO WRITE OR DRAW!

PENS & PAPER

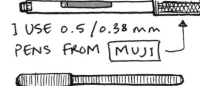

I USE 0.5 / 0.38 mm PENS FROM MUJI

PILOT V SIGN PENS

GENERALLY LOTS OF TEXT, AND I USE PICTURES TO ILLUSTRATE KEY CONCEPTS

DON'T UNDERSTAND

BORED

TIRED!

NO PROBLEM
FINISH OFF OTHER NOTES, PREPARE FOR THE NEXT ONE, OR JUST SKETCH THE AUDIENCE!

TOMBOW DUAL BRUSH PENS FOR SHADING (THANKS, EVA-LOTTA!)

HARD-BACK NOTEBOOKS GIVE YOU SOMETHING TO LEAN ON (A4)

 TIPS FOR **LISTENING**

SKETCHNOTES ARE ALL ABOUT OBSERVATION AND LISTENING... IF THEY TALK TOO FAST, YOU JUST HAVE TO LISTEN FASTER!

YOU NEED THE **EARS** OF THE **CHEETAH**

TIPS FOR **DRAWING**

USE A PEN (NOT A PENCIL)

–

THINK ABOUT STRUCTURE AND USE ANY CUES FROM THE SPEAKER

–

YOU CAN ADD THE COLOUR & SHADING LATER... IT'S OK!

IT DRIVES ME NUTS WHEN I HAVE TO START A NEW PAGE JUST FOR A SMALL BIT OF SKETCHING!

AND ONCE, I WAS AT A CONFERENCE WHERE THEY TURNED OFF ALL THE LIGHTS!

 I'M PROUD WHEN PEOPLE USE SKETCHNOTES I'VE MADE...

...BEING INVITED...

...TO MAKE NOTES...

FRAMED COPY

DR ALEX BATEMAN SANGER INSTITUTE

GET IN TOUCH

in 🐦 📷

francis rowland

CHAPTER 7

SKETCHNOTING SKILLS and TECHNIQUES

IT'S TIME TO BUILD YOUR VISUAL NOTE TAKING TOOLBOX.

SO FAR YOU'VE LEARNED:

- ☑ What sketchnotes are
- ☑ Why you should create them
- ☑ How to create sketchnotes
- ☑ How to personalize sketchnotes

SKILLS & TECHNIQUES

In this chapter, you'll learn:

- → How to draw using the five basic shapes
- → How to draw people simply and quickly
- → How to draw faces and expressions
- → How to create four different typefaces
- → How to improve your penmanship
- → How to draw various visual elements
- → How to build your mind's visual library
- → Which tools to use for sketchnoting
- → Tips for sharing your sketchnotes

ideas NOT ART.

BEFORE YOU LEARN TO DRAW VISUAL ELEMENTS
remember that sketchnotes are about capturing and sharing ideas, not art. Even bad drawings can convey good ideas.

······─────────────······

If you're not an artist or feel you can't draw well,

YOU CAN CREATE SKETCHNOTES!

The following exercises are designed to help you start slowly and build on your successes. You can do it!

the FIVE

BASIC ←·······

Elements

OF DRAWING

★ DRAW ALMOST ANYTHING ★
WITH THESE 5 ELEMENTS.

THAT'S RIGHT! You can draw pretty much anything you can imagine with just five basic drawing elements.

The FIVE BASIC DRAWING ELEMENTS:

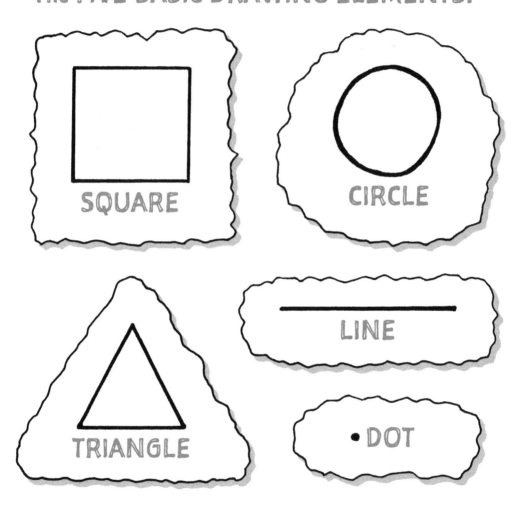

SQUARE

CIRCLE

LINE

TRIANGLE

• DOT

THIS SIMPLER WAY of creating images is often a relief for non-artists who want to add drawings to their sketchnotes but think they can't draw.

FOR THE IDEA-FOCUSED DRAWINGS you want to add to sketchnotes, drawing complex ideas by building them with simple squares, triangles, circles, lines, and dots is a handy technique. Can you spot the five elements in each of the following figures?

House   Car   iPhone   Book

Pencil   Laptop   Factory

Earth   Satellite   Radio   TV

Cat   Dog   Lightsaber   Robot

↓

**RATHER
THAN CREATE**
museum-quality
ILLUSTRATIONS,

focus **INSTEAD** on
**QUICKLY CREATING
SIMPLE DRAWINGS**
of the **IDEAS
IN YOUR HEAD**
using the 5 basic elements.

COMPARE THESE 10 ITEMS

5 FANCY ILLUSTRATIONS	5 SIMPLE DRAWINGS

Woman   Woman

Laptop   Tree   Laptop   Tree

Pie Chart   Book   Pie Chart   Book

Fancy illustrations by Greg Newman   *Simple drawings by Mike Rohde*

FANCY ILLUSTRATIONS AND SIMPLE DRAWINGS
convey the same ideas, but simpler drawings are quicker to create.
When you're working live, speed and effectiveness are *critical*.

FIVE BASIC ELEMENTS Exercise

Now it's time for you to draw! In the grid below, use the five basic elements—square, circle, triangle, line, and dot—to create drawings of each word in the grid. If you get stuck, skip to the next word.

HOUSE	CAR	CLOCK	BOOK
LAPTOP	COFFEE MUG	BOAT	IGLOO
CAT	DOG	TRUCK	TRAIN
TRACTOR	LIGHTBULB	EARTH	SATURN
MOUNTAIN	TREE	HAMMER	WRENCH

FISH	BIRD	BUG	ROBOT
FLASHLIGHT	CAMERA	SUBMARINE	SANDWICH
HEADPHONES	MILK JUG	BATTERY	TV
DVD	TV REMOTE	MINIVAN	BIKE
BASEBALL CAP	T-SHIRT	SHOES	TRASH CAN
HAMBURGER	PEN	PENCIL	WATCH

DRAWING PEOPLE

Drawing people quickly is a great skill to learn. There are many ways to draw people — I'll show you the two quickest ways.

THE STAR METHOD

This method is used by professional graphic recorders for its speed and simplicity. Follow these four easy steps:

1 Draw the head

2 Draw a star-shaped body

3 Complete the body

4 Add faces, hair, clothes, etc.

THE GRAY METHOD

Dave Gray taught me another way of drawing people using a rectangle, an oval, and several lines. I love this way of drawing people because it's quick and allows for embellishment if I have extra time. Follow these six easy steps:

1 Draw a Body

Start by drawing the person's body as a rectangle, which can be straight up and down for a formal pose or at any angle for an active pose. The position of this rectangle sets much of the body's attitude and direction.

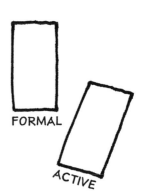

FORMAL

ACTIVE

2 Draw a Neck

Next, draw a neck as a line at the top of the rectangle. Keep the neck short.

3 Draw a Head

Draw a head as a circle or an oval at the top of the neck line. Make sure there is enough room inside the head for a face.

④ Draw Legs

Using lines, add legs to the body because legs suggest the body's gesture more clearly than arms. Bend the legs at the knees as needed. Use simple lines for the feet.

⑤ Draw Arms

Next, draw arms in relation to the rest of the body, bending at the elbows. A simple line works well for hands.

⑥ Draw a Face

Finally, use simple lines and dots to draw eyes, a nose, and a mouth. For the nose, a simple line works well and can be pointed in the direction your person is looking.

★ EMBELLISH!

Have fun adding more details to your person once the basic structure has been created.

DRAWING PEOPLE Exercise

In the grid below, use the Gray Method to draw people. I've written some suggestions in the open grids to challenge you a bit. Try adding clothes, shoes, hats, and other details — have fun!

STANDING	RUNNING
WALKING	JUMPING

SITTING	ON THE PHONE	DANCING
DAD & SON WALKING	BACKPACKER	READING A BOOK
TENNIS PLAYER	KUNG FU MASTER	MASTER CHEF

DRAWING FACES

My friend Austin Kleon has a way of drawing faces using a few straight and curved lines for eyebrows and mouths, a triangular nose, and dots for eyes. Using these elements in a bingo grid, you can quickly create nine different facial expressions:

DRAWING FACES Exercise

Now it's your turn to create faces using Austin's approach:

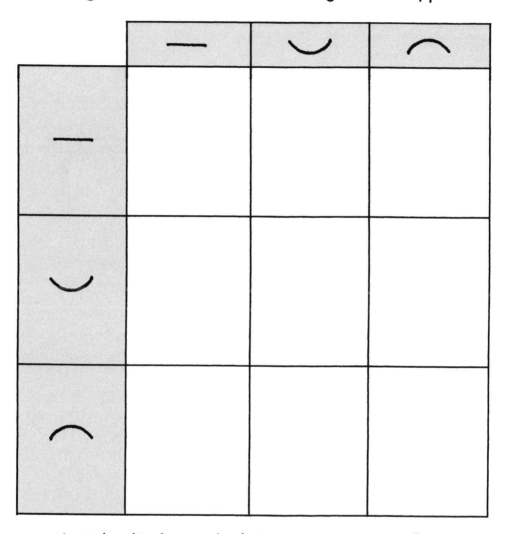

Next, try that same technique on some blank faces:

DRAW MORE FACES Exercise

Now it's time to create more faces. I've provided a few eye and mouth options, but feel free to make up your own.

EYES

MOUTHS

BIFF

BUFFY

MOZZY

TEX

FRED

BIANCA

BOB

FRANKIE

WHAT OTHER FACIAL EXPRESSIONS CAN YOU CREATE?

Drawing

TYPE

TYPE

TYPE

TYPE

DRAWING TYPE

A great way to immediately improve your plain text notes is to emphasize words with hand-drawn typography. In fact, you can create bolder or larger letterforms by hand in four easy ways:

SINGLE-LINE LETTERING

Using a single line, these clean headlines can draw attention to a section you'd like to emphasize in your sketchnotes. Plus, drawing single-line lettering is *easy* and *quick*.

SMALL LETTERING

Large Lettering

All caps, small, single-line letters are great for establishing sections within a sketchnote.

Uppercase and lowercase single-line lettering is especially effective when used for headlines.

WHEN DRAWING TYPE, JUST RELAX, AND LET THE LETTERS FLOW ONTO THE PAGE.

When creating single-line lettering, slow down and deliberately create each character:

ABCDEFGHIJKLMNO

The great thing about learning the single-line type method is that many of these type creation methods are based on it.

TWO-LINE LETTERING

By drawing two lines in parallel, you can create bolder type. You can also draw the type as a single line, adding a second line next to it.

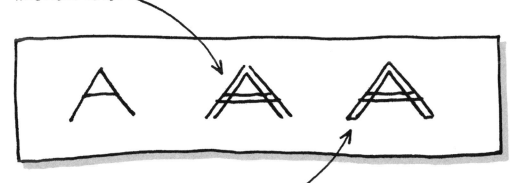

Next, you can close the ends of each character with a small line, and then fill in the gap with ink for bold, black letters.

DRAW YOUR LETTERS WITH CONFIDENCE. NEVER HURRY.

TRIPLE-LINE LETTERING

This bold lettering style begins with a single-lined letter, and then two lines are added on either side of the center line.

As with two-line lettering, you can close the ends of each character with a small line, and then fill in the gap with ink for very bold, black letters.

START SIMPLE & BUILD UP

Using the single-line lettering method allows you to quickly convert your letters to two- or triple-line lettering, simply by adding more lines, even at a later time.

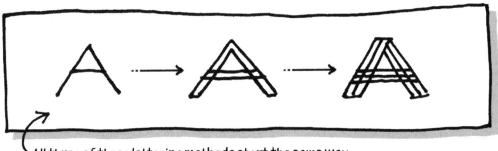

All three of these lettering methods start the same way.

BLOCK LETTERING

The block lettering approach requires a little more practice, skill, and time. When used properly, block lettering is a nice way to create a strong impression. Block lettering works well on title pages or when you want to emphasize a key point.

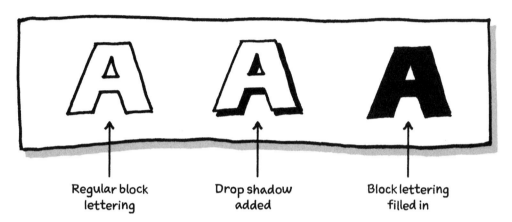

Regular block lettering

Drop shadow added

Block lettering filled in

WITH ALL of these hand-drawn lettering approaches, you may need to start the first few letters and leave the rest for later. This is fine — just remember to finish the words you've started drawing when the sketchnote is completed.

Started but incomplete

Completed at a later time

DRAWING TYPE Exercise

Practicing hand-lettering techniques will help you quickly create type for your sketchnotes in a meeting. Use these pages to practice creating single-line, two-line, triple-line, and block lettering.

SINGLE-LINE LETTERING:

ABCabc

TWO-LINE LETTERING:

ABCabc

TRIPLE-LINE LETTERING:

ABCabc

BLOCK LETTERING:

ABCabc

the **PEN** IS MIGHTIER THAN THE *Sword.*

PENMANSHIP

Although large typographic elements work great for highlighting sections and ideas, you'll still need legible handwriting to capture detailed ideas in your sketchnotes.

10 YEARS AGO I wrote only in ALL CAPS block letters after abandoning lowercase handwriting. It took me months of practicing lowercase letter writing to get comfortable with it again. So, if your handwriting is rough and illegible, you can change it! Just take it slow and keep working on it.

My old ALL CAPS handwriting   My lowercase handwriting

MIKE'S PENMANSHIP TIPS:
Here are a few tips that help me when I need clear, legible writing:

1 Practice
Just a few minutes a day does the trick.

2 Slow Down
Focus on each letter, one at a time. Don't rush!

3 Relax
Loosen your grip and relax your arm tension as you write.

DRAWING VISUAL ELEMENTS

Visual elements add interest to your sketchnotes and can be a variety of shapes and sizes. Here are a few you may find useful to learn as part of your practice routines:

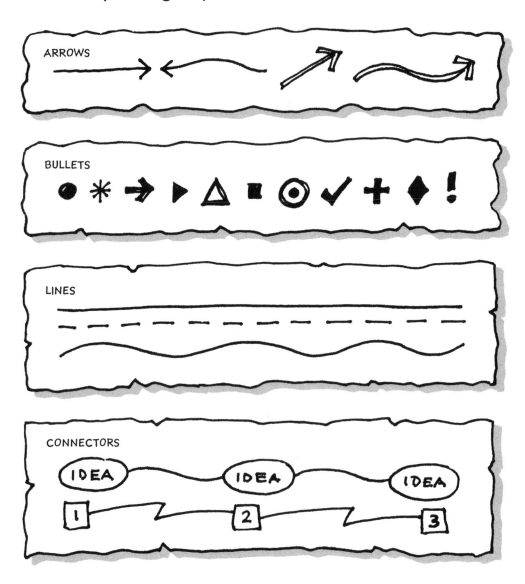

ARROWS

BULLETS

LINES

CONNECTORS

IDEA — IDEA — IDEA

1   2   3

BUILD A VISUAL LIBRARY

As you learn and practice drawing all the visual elements you've explored in this chapter, you're actually building a visual library of items.

Learning these techniques is a great way to add selections to your visual library. Another activity is to challenge yourself to draw items from memory when you have some downtime.

FOR EXAMPLE, using the exercise sheets in this chapter, use your memory and draw objects from your kitchen and office. Imagine your toaster, coffee maker, computer, or stapler, and draw it.

Push your mind to think of small, obscure items and draw each one in the book using the five basic drawing elements. This visual exercise challenges you to imagine things in your mind's eye and then draw them as simple objects.

KEEP PRACTICING

Once you've filled the visual library exercises in this book, keep your mind in practice by creating new visual library objects using blank sheets of paper, sticky notes, a pocket notebook — even the back of junk mail envelopes.

with a
WELL-STOCKED
VISUAL
LIBRARY
IN YOUR MEMORY,
drawing ideas
and objects
BECOMES EASIER.

VISUAL LIBRARY Exercise: Kitchen

In the grid below, draw as many items from your kitchen from memory as you can recall. Remember to use the five basic elements to draw the images you're seeing in your head.

VISUAL LIBRARY Exercise: Office

In the grid below, draw as many items from your office from memory as you can recall. Remember to use the five basic elements to draw the images you're seeing in your head.

DRAWING METAPHORS

Metaphors are figures of speech that use the attributes of a known idea to describe another, apparently unrelated idea. Good metaphors lean on vivid imagery.

METAPHORS SHOULD BE BOLD & FUNNY

The most successful metaphors I've captured as sketchnotes have been bold and a bit over the top. I like to use humorous ideas for drawn metaphors because funny images are surprising and more likely to stick in your head.

WORLD PEACE

WORLD WIDE WEB

BUCKET LISTS

THE KEY TO CREATING METAPHORS

Let your imagination have free rein when you're sketching metaphors. Don't be afraid to use crazy, silly, or wild drawings for your metaphors. The most absurd drawings I've created for sketchnotes are often the most memorable.

JOHN LOST HIS HEAD

TIME FLIES

HOT HEAD

Seek out the
SILLIEST, CRAZIEST, WILDEST IDEAS as METAPHORS.

THE MOST BIZARRE IDEAS CAPTURE ATTENTION AND ARE UNFORGETTABLE.

TOOLS *for* SKETCHNOTING

Any paper or notebook, pencil or pen will work just fine for sketchnoting. However, there are pens and papers that work better for some than others.

I use pocket-sized Moleskine sketchbooks because they're small and can take a beating in my pocket or backpack.

MOLESKINE SKETCHBOOK

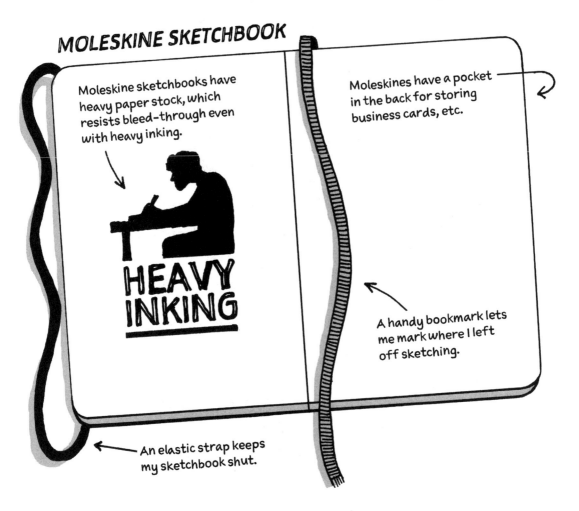

Moleskine sketchbooks have heavy paper stock, which resists bleed-through even with heavy inking.

HEAVY INKING

Moleskines have a pocket in the back for storing business cards, etc.

A handy bookmark lets me mark where I left off sketching.

An elastic strap keeps my sketchbook shut.

A Moleskine's two-page spreads work well for the linear sketchnotes I create. Here's a sample:

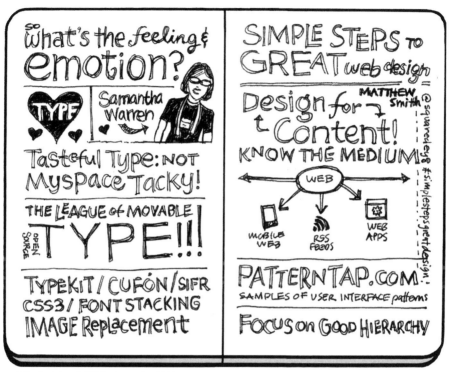

Mike Rohde • SXSW Interactive 2010

MY STYLE features high-contrast, black-and-white typography and drawings, so I use a bold, 0.7mm gel pen.

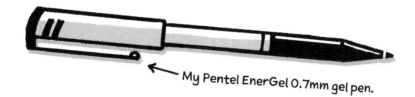

My Pentel EnerGel 0.7mm gel pen.

OTHER NOTEBOOK & PEN OPTIONS

Some sketchnoters prefer square or spiral notebooks. Others use finer black lines as a base and then amplify their sketchnotes afterward with colored markers, colored pencils, or even watercolor paints.

SPIRAL-BOUND SKETCHBOOK

Amanda Wright • Don Norman

You can find a wide variety of paper types in spiral notebooks to handle ink, markers, and even watercolor paint.

Spiral notebooks are great for laying flat on tables.

Spiral notebooks can also be flipped open for easy access to any page in the book.

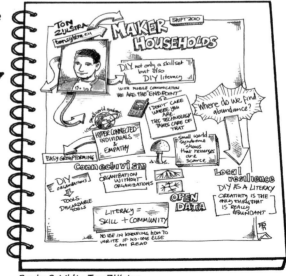

Bauke Schildt • Ton Zijlstra

PEN OPTIONS include gel, ball point, or felt tips (0.3 to 0.5mm fine point), which dry quickly. Highlight your sketchnotes with felt-tipped markers or colored pencils.

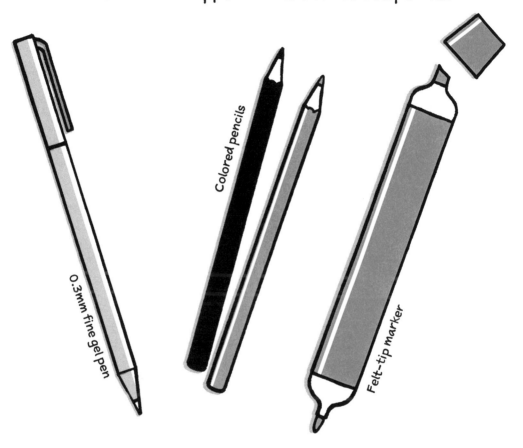

0.3mm fine gel pen

Colored pencils

Felt-tip marker

The books and pens you choose are up to you. Experiment with a variety of book styles, pens, and markers until you find the right combination that works best for you.

SHARING SKETCHNOTES

Sharing sketchnotes can be as simple as shooting and posting a photo with your smartphone or as complex as making high-resolution scans on your desktop computer.
I often share my work both ways.

SMARTPHONES

Smartphones are convenient to carry anywhere and can create highly detailed photos for backup and sharing.

By sharing your sketchnotes using the camera on your phone and posting them to your favorite social media site, you're drawing others in to enjoy your work right away.

To help others understand and share your sketchnotes, add a brief but clear description of the event and a link to your work.

Making your sketchnotes easy to comprehend and share can make what you've created more attractive for readers to check out and even share with the world.

DIGITAL CAMERAS

Another option is to carry a high-end, point-and-shoot pocket or DSLR camera with you to capture photos of your work to share at a later time. I've found pocket point-and-shoot cameras have a good trade-off between quality and portability when I'm sketchnoting at an event.

SCANNERS

A quality flatbed scanner produces the best images, especially if the end result of your sketchnotes is a PDF document or a printed booklet.

I prefer a small scanner powered from a USB cable. This allows me to carry it along to an event if needed. I scan my work as PNG files, which I can convert to PDF files or send to a printer for final print production.

I use Photoshop to tweak the contrast and levels, and save a final file with each spread of sketchnotes on a layer. This makes it easy to work with and export a large batch of sketchnotes.

DRAWING LICENCE

CHRIS SHIPTON

CARTOONIST

OXFORD, UK — CHRISSHIPTON.CO.UK

EQUIPMENT:
I PREFER MOLESKINE BOOKS BUT AM GIVING LEUCHTURM1917 A GO... AND FOR SKETCHNOTING I LIKE A PILOT VSIGN BACKED UP WITH A FABER CASTELL PITT PEN (B) AND A FEW MAGIC MARKERS...

ABOUT ME:

I HAVE ALWAYS DRAWN STUFF

AND LIKE MANY WAS REGULARLY TOLD OFF FOR IT THROUGHOUT MY EDUCATION

AT ART SCHOOL...

I HAVE A DEGREE IN DRAWING YOU KNOW...

TEENAGE YEARS...

GIVE ME THAT PEN!

NO!

ONE MANS DEFACED PHYSICS BOOK IS ANOTHERS SKETCHNOTES!

LATER...

SKETCH WHATS?

CLICK CLICK

OUT | IN

IMAGINE MY SURPRISE WHEN ONE DAY, IDLY SURFING THE NET I DISCOVERED SKETCHNOTES WERE AN ACTUAL THING!!

NOW MY JOB IS GRAPHIC RECORDING!

AND AS A CARTOONIST...

OR ILLUSTRATOR

OR GRAPHIC FACILITATOR!!

GRAPHIC RECORDING OR LIVE ILLUSTRATION OR MASSIVE SKETCHNOTES!

TOP TIP #1 BEFORE DOING ANY DRAWING

WARM UP FIRST!

→ SCRIBBLE
→ DRAW SQUIGGLES
→ DRAW SOMEONE NEAR YOU!

REMEMBER OLD PHONES? AND HEAVILY DOODLED PHONE BOOKS?

PHONE BOOK

PROTO-SKETCHNOTES!

ARE YOU DRAWING ME?

 me

HELLO!

MY NAME IS KYLE STEED

I LIVE IN  The LONE STATE Texas

AMANDA

WITH MY WIFE

 & OUR TWO

← BEN

CRAZY DOGS

SAM ↗

PAYS THE BILLS

HAND-DRAWN

ILLUSTRATIONS AND DESIGN

LOOSE LEAF

I PREFER THE MICRON PENS WHEN I'M DRAWING

MICRON .03

YOU ALSO CAN'T GO WRONG WITH THIS GUY

FIELD NOTES

FIELD NOTES

MOLESKINE

JUST have fun

↖ THE BEST ADVICE I CAN GIVE SOMEONE

FIND ME ON TWITTER
@KYLESTEED

CHECK OUT MY WEBSITE
KYLESTEED.COM

CONGRATULATIONS!

You've made it to the end of *The Sketchnote Handbook!* Now you have a better idea of what sketchnotes are and how to create them.

Here are a few details to remember:

★ **START SLOWLY**
Use just a quarter of the page to start and expand as you improve your skills.

★ **BUILD ON SUCCESS**
Try a few techniques and be happy with your progress as you continue to improve. Go easy on yourself!

★ **LISTEN UP**
Manage distractions, listen closely, and concentrate. The more you practice listening, the better you'll get.

★ **DRAW SIMPLY**
Use the 5 basic elements to draw simple shapes, just like kids do. Bad drawings can still convey good ideas!

★ **EXPLORE**
Find your own way as you learn to sketchnote. Everyone has a unique way of forming ideas and capturing them.

★ **SHARE**
Share those sketchnotes! You're invited to share your work at *The Sketchnote Handbook* group on Flickr:

www.flickr.com/groups/thesketchnotehandbook

GUESS WHAT?

YOU CAN DO THIS.

Yes, you really can!

SO GET Sketchnoting!

WE'RE ON THIS JOURNEY TOGETHER.

INDEX